Victims of Bullying

ISSUES
(formerly Issues for the Nineties)

Volume 13

Editor

Craig Donnellan

Independence
Educational Publishers
Cambridge

First published by Independence
PO Box 295
Cambridge CB1 3XP
England

British Library Cataloguing in Publication Data
Victims of Bullying – (Issues Series)
I. Donnellan, Craig II. Series
371.5'8

ISBN 1 86168 153 4

Printed in Great Britain
The Burlington Press
Cambridge

Typeset by
Claire Boyd

Cover
The illustration on the front cover is by
Pumpkin House.

CONTENTS

Chapter One: Bullying at School

Chapter Two: Bullying in the Workplace

Introduction

Victims of Bullying is the thirteenth volume in the **Issues** series. The aim of this series is to offer up-to-date information about important issues in our world.

Victims of Bullying looks at bullying at school and in the workplace.

The information comes from a wide variety of sources and includes:
Government reports and statistics
Newspaper reports and features
Magazine articles and surveys
Literature from lobby groups
and charitable organisations.

It is hoped that, as you read about the many aspects of the issues explored in this book, you will critically evaluate the information presented. It is important that you decide whether you are being presented with facts or opinions. Does the writer give a biased or an unbiased report? If an opinion is being expressed, do you agree with the writer?

Victims of Bullying offers a useful starting-point for those who need convenient access to information about the many issues involved. However, it is only a starting-point. At the back of the book is a list of organisations which you may want to contact for further information.

*****

Bullying

Information from ChildLine

What is bullying?

Bullying can mean many different things. These are some ways children and young people have described bullying:

- being called names
- being teased
- being pushed or pulled about
- being hit or attacked
- having your bag and other possessions taken and thrown around
- having rumours spread about you
- being ignored and left out
- being forced to hand over money or possessions
- being attacked because of your religion or colour.

What does it feel like to be bullied?

Bullying hurts. It makes you scared and upset. It can make you so worried that you can't work well at school. Some children have told us they have skipped school to get away from it. It can make you feel that you are no good, that there is something wrong with you. Bullies can make you feel that it's your fault.

Why do bullies do it?

- They have their own problems – they may feel upset or angry or feel that they don't fit in – perhaps they have problems at home
- Maybe they get bullied themselves, perhaps by someone in their own family or other adults
- They're scared of getting picked on so they do it first
- They want to show off and seem tough
- Many don't like themselves and so take it out on someone else.

Sometimes adults bully too

Adults can and do bully children – mums and dads, other family members, and teachers, for example. They may do it by making you feel bad in front of other people, by shouting and scaring you, by teasing or making fun of you. It can be very difficult to do something about it, especially if the adult is the one you would normally go to about being bullied. Don't give up – find a sympathetic adult, perhaps another teacher and talk to them about the problem.

How to stop the bullying

If you are being bullied, you can do something about it.
You can make a difference!

- TELL, TELL, TELL
- Practise what you want to say
- Keep a note or diary of what is happening
- Don't give up
- Ask your parents to visit the school
- Talk over what to do with a friend, a teacher, your mum or dad or someone you trust
- Remember that teachers have to listen carefully when a child tells them about being bullied.

Remember – it's right to tell an adult that you are being bullied and to ask for their help. But you don't have to let them take over. You can talk with them about what you would like to happen.

Are you a bully?

If you are bullying, or have bullied someone, it is a good idea to get some help. Who could you speak to? A teacher? Your parents? ChildLine?

Helping a friend

Maybe you're not being bullied, but you know someone who is – perhaps that person is not even a good friend, but a class-mate or someone from another class? Have you ever stood around and noticed that someone was being bullied, but you weren't sure what, if anything, you could do? Or thought that nothing you could do would make a difference?

Don't ignore bullying. You can help. Don't let the bullies get away with thinking that no one will do anything. Here are a few things you can do, and a couple that you can't:

- Don't rush over and take them on – it might not be safe and you don't want other people to think you are a bully
- Let a teacher or other adult know what's happening
- Try to be a friend to the person being bullied
- Refuse to join in
- Try to be friendly to the bully, but even if you can't be friends, being kind can sometimes help the bully stop bullying
- Sometimes you can't sort it out yourself. Ask an adult for help.

Your school can help

Your school should be clearly saying NO to bullying.

- Get everyone in your school involved in tackling bullying, not just the teachers, but other pupils, dinner ladies and playground assistants.
- Find out how much bullying goes on in your school. Get together with other pupils and a teacher to organise a questionnaire about bullying (you can make sure that no one reads the individual answers by putting them in a locked box). Once you have received all the answers, you can write up a short report for everyone to read.
- Make sure your school has a good selection of anti-bullying books and other information in its library. Suggest that the school runs an anti-bullying week.
- Talk to your teachers about having assemblies and discussions in class about bullying – classes could produce posters, pictures, poems, stories, plays which could

be shared with the rest of the school.

- Children need to feel safe at break time and lunchtime in the playgrounds – are there lots of things to do and supervisors around?
- Get your school to put up ChildLine posters.
- In some schools, older children help younger children if they are being bullied. Some have set up 'peer counselling' schemes run by the pupils to help children who are being bullied, but also to help children who bully. If you would like more information about peer counselling, ask your teachers. ChildLine can also give you some information about it.

ChildLine can help

ChildLine is the free telephone helpline for children and young

people. You can ring any time of day, any day of the year. It's free and it's confidential – that means that no one else will know about the conversation unless you decide to tell them. The call will not show up on the family phone bill, although it may if you use a mobile or cable phone. Sometimes it's hard to get through, because the lines are all busy. But keep trying, you will get through eventually.

Many children call ChildLine to talk about bullying. Last year, over 10,000 children called. If you want to talk to someone, you can speak to one of our counsellors.

Where can you go for help and information?

ChildLine
Helpline 0800 1111 (open 24 hours a day, every day).

Kidscape
Helpline – 0171 730 3300 (open Mon and Wed 9.30am – 5.30pm). Kidscape produces leaflets and booklets about bullying.

Anti-bullying campaign
Helpline – 0171 378 1446 (open Mon-Fri 9.30am – 5.30pm). They also produce leaflets and information for parents.

• The above information is an extract from ChildLine's web site which can be found at www.childline.org.uk Alternatively, see page 41 for their address details.

© ChildLine

Some people say . . .

- 'Bullying is just part of growing up . . .' It isn't. You don't have to put up with it. Adults don't put up with being hit and shouted at when they go to work. You shouldn't have to, either.
- 'If you hit back, you won't get bullied again . . .' Don't believe it. It may work sometimes, but it is just as likely to make things worse.
- 'Only victims get bullied . . .' It is not true that some people are more likely to be bullied than others. Although some people are bullied because they may be different in some way (they have a disability, are from another country, or speak with a different accent), many other children are bullied without any obvious reason. Don't forget that bullies have sometimes been bullied themselves.
- 'My school says there's no bullying here . . .' Your school may be very lucky to have no bullying problem at the moment, but most schools recognise that bullying does go on, and many are doing something about it. If your school is ignoring bullying, talk to your mum or dad about what to do. They might be able to talk to other parents, and meet with the Head to try to tackle the problem.

The emotional cost of bullying

Information from the Royal College of Psychiatrists

What is bullying?

Bullying happens when a child is picked on by another child, or group of children. It is hurtful and deliberate. It can happen in many different ways. Children who bully may:

- hit or punch another child.
- kick them.
- trip them up.
- take or spoil their things.
- call them names.
- tease them.
- give them nasty looks.
- threaten them.
- make racist remarks about them.
- spread nasty rumours or stories about them.
- not let them join in play or games.
- not talk to them – 'send them to Coventry'.

Victims find it difficult to defend themselves. Bullying usually happens again and again. It goes on for a long time, unless something is done about it.

How common is bullying?

Bullying is very common and probably happens in all schools. Recent surveys in this country have shown that 1 in 4 primary school pupils, and 1 in 10 secondary school pupils, are being bullied.

Why does it happen?

There is no single reason why some children become bullies, and others are bullied by them. Children who are aggressive are more likely to become bullies. Often they have seen, or been a victim of, violence at home. Typically, they pick on children who appear different in some way – those who are quiet, shy, alone at playtime and unable to defend themselves. Children who stammer, who have a disability or who have special educational needs are also more likely to be bullied.

Schools vary in how much bullying there is and how they deal with it. Some schools have a clear policy on bullying. They make sure that all teachers, parents, and children know about it. They make it clear that they won't allow bullying or aggressive behaviour. Schools that have these policies, and who take every incident of bullying seriously, tend to have less bullying.

What effects does bullying have?

Being bullied can seriously affect a child's physical and mental health. They will often suffer in silence. They lack confidence, feel bad about themselves, have few friends and spend playtime alone. They may find it hard to face going to school and difficult to concentrate on their work. They may complain of various physical symptoms as a result of their upset and worry. Others become very anxious, find it hard to sleep and may feel depressed or even suicidal. These problems can carry on long after the bullying has stopped.

Who and what can help?

Parents:

Listen – One of the most important things you can do is to listen to your child if they say they are being bullied. Children often become tearful and upset when telling someone about it.

Take your child seriously – Many children suffer in silence for a long time before they tell anyone. They are often ashamed, embarrassed and may believe that they deserve it. Many children are frightened of telling because they fear their bullies will find out and hurt them even more. It can take great courage to tell an adult.

Do not blame the child – Being bullied is not their fault (although they may think it is).

Reassure them that they were right to tell.

Do not promise to keep the bullying a secret – Something must be done about it. Reassure your child that you, and the teachers, will make sure that things do not get worse because they have told you. Tell the school so they can stop it. Teachers don't always know that a child is being bullied. Make sure that there is an active anti-bullying programme in the school. Include your child when you are deciding how to tackle the problem.

Talk with your child and work out ways of solving the problem – For example,

work out some practical ways they can use to stop the bullying. You might discuss what they should say back if they are called names, or where it's safe to go at playtime.

School:
Bullying happens in every school, so it is important that each school has an effective anti-bullying programme. Good intentions aren't enough. Both pupils and staff need to act when they see a child being bullied. We know that these programmes are very effective. Every school can obtain an anti-bullying pack from the Department for Education and Employment. There are a number of agencies that can offer advice and help in how to set up effective programmes (see below).

Other professionals who can help
Children whose health has been affected may benefit from some specialist help from the GP, school doctor, a social worker or an educational psychologist who will be able to offer help and advice. Children with emotional problems quite often need these treated directly even if the school has managed to stop the bullying. A child and adolescent psychiatrist will be able to advise you as to which kind of help will be most effective.

Your GP or another professional can refer you to your child and adolescent mental health service with a team including child psychiatrists, psychologists, social workers, psychotherapists and specialist nurses.

Sources of further information
MacLeod, M. & Morris, S. (1996) *Why Me? Children Talking to Childline about Bullying.* Available from ChildLine, Freepost 1111, London N1 OBR. For their free and confidential telephone service for children, call 0800 1111. Web site www.ChildLine.org.uk

Department for Education and Employment (1994) *Bullying: Don't Suffer in Silence. An Anti-Bullying Pack for Schools.* London: HMSO.

The Anti-Bullying Campaign for Parents and Children provides telephone advice and support. 10 Borough High Street, London SE1 9QQ. Telephone 020 7378 1448.

Kidscape provide advice, run training courses and produce helpful booklets and information about bullying. 2 Grosvenor Gardens, London SW1W ODH. Telephone 020 7730 3300.

The Mental Health & Growing Up series contains 36 factsheets on a range of common mental health problems, including discipline, behavioural problems and conduct disorder, and stimulant medication. To order the pack, contact Book Sales at the Royal College of Psychiatrists, 17 Belgrave Square, London SW1X 8PG. Telephone 020 7235 2351, ext. 146; fax 020 7245 1231; e-mail booksales@rcpsych.ac.uk

Bullying

Information from Kidscape
What can I do if I am being bullied?

Your school may already have a way of dealing with bullying. For example, some schools:

- have anti-bullying guidelines and procedures for dealing with incidents
- encourage anyone who is being bullied, or has witnessed bullying, to tell someone about it
- have 'bully boxes' where people can leave notes about what is happening
- have student meetings or even 'courts' where problems like bullying are discussed and dealt with
- have specially assigned students or teachers who are there to help.

If your school has an anti-bullying system, use it to get help. If you're not sure how it works then talk to a teacher.

Some schools ignore bullying but don't *become resigned to being a victim.* You can still help yourself and ask others to help you.

- Tell a friend what is happening. Ask him or her to help you. It will be harder for the bully to pick on you if you have a friend with you for support.
- Try to ignore the bullying or say 'No' really firmly, then turn and walk away. Don't worry if people think you are running away. Remember, it is very hard for the bully to go on bullying someone who won't stand still to listen.
- Try not to show that you are upset or angry. Bullies love to get a reaction – it's 'fun'. If you can keep calm and hide your emotions, they might get bored and leave you alone. As one teenager said to us, 'they can't bully you if you don't care'.
- Don't fight back if you can help it. Most bullies are bigger or stronger than you. If you fight back you could make the situation

N early everyone is bullied at some time in their lives: by brothers and sisters, by neighbours, by adults or by other children. If you are being bullied, you may feel scared, vulnerable and quite alone but you owe it to yourself to try and sort out the situation so that the the bullying stops. Remember, no one deserves to be bullied.

It is surprising that all sorts of people who are now very successful adults were bullied when they were young. It is encouraging to know that it is possible to succeed, in spite of being tormented at school. All of these well-known people were bullied at school: Phil Collins, Harrison Ford, Mel Gibson, Tom Cruise, Michelle Pfeiffer, Frank Bruno and many others.

For some, the bullying went on for years; for others it was less frequent. All of them feel that bullying is wrong and that it was not their fault, but the fault of the bully looking for a victim.

worse, get hurt or be blamed for starting the trouble.

- It's not worth getting hurt to keep possessions or money. If you feel threatened, give the bullies what they want. Property can be replaced, you can't.

- Try to think up funny or clever replies in advance. Make a joke of it. Replies don't have to be wonderfully brilliant or clever but it helps to have an answer ready. Practise saying them in the mirror at home. Using prepared replies works best if the bully is not too threatening and just needs to be put off. The bully might just decide that you are too clever to pick on.

- Try to avoid being alone in the places where you know the bully is likely to pick on you. This might mean changing your route to school, avoiding parts of the playground, or only using common rooms or lavatories when other people are there. It's not fair that you have to do this, but it might put the bully off.

- Sometimes asking the bully to repeat what they said can put

---

Often, people don't tell about bullying because they are afraid the bully will find out and things will get worse

---

them off. Often bullies are not brave enought to repeat the remark exactly so they tone it down. If they repeat it, you will have made them do something they hadn't planned on and this gives you some control of the situation.

- Keep a diary of what is happening. Write down the details of the incidents and your feelings. When you do decide to tell someone, a written record of the bullying makes it easier to prove what has been going on.

Who can I tell?

Usually it's difficult to sort out the bullying on your own or even with the help of friends. You should think

seriously about telling an adult. It's the only way to get the bullying stopped.

If you need help, don't be embarrassed about asking. Everyone needs help sometimes and asking for help to stop bullying doesn't mean that you are weak or a failure.

Telling about bullying isn't 'telling tales' or 'grassing'. You have the right to be safe from attacks and harassment and you should not be silent when you are being tormented and hurt.

Often, people don't tell about bullying because they are afraid the bully will find out and things will get worse. This is a natural fear but schools can put a stop to bullying without the bully learning who told, especially if the bully has several victims.

Even if the bully does find out, it is better to have things out in the open.

- The above information is from Kidscape's website which can be found at www.kidscape.org.uk

© Kidscape

School children fear bullying and violence

Information from MORI

More than a third of school pupils (36 per cent) have been bullied in the past twelve months, a quarter (26 per cent) have been threatened with violence in school and 13 per cent have been physically attacked, according to a major survey by the 150,000-strong Association of Teachers and Lecturers (ATL).

The survey of 2,600 pupils aged 11 to 16 in England and Wales was conducted by leading opinion pollsters, MORI, for ATL and is published today as delegates arrive in Belfast for the start of the Association's annual conference. Conference delegates will be debating the issue of social inclusion

on Wednesday (19 April) and will be disturbed to hear that 30 per cent of pupils feel their teachers are not aware of bullying in school while

one in eleven (9 per cent) report that they have missed school because of their fear of violence.

Younger pupils are twice as likely to experience bullying than older pupils. More than half of 11-year-olds (51 per cent) report incidents compared to a quarter of 15 and 16-year-olds (26 per cent). However, older pupils are more likely to feel their teachers are not aware of bullying with two in five pupils (41 per cent) believing this to be the case.

The same survey also found that pupils' concerns for personal safety extended beyond the school gates as a quarter (26 per cent) said they are worried about travelling to and from school. Girls are more likely than boys to be concerned about safety as 30 per cent said they hold such fears compared to 22 per cent of boys. Girls are also more worried about violence (44 per cent compared to 39 per cent of boys) even though boys are more likely to have been threatened (33 per cent compared to 19 per cent of girls) while three times as many boys than girls (19 per cent boys, 6 per cent girls) report being physically attacked at school.

Regional variations reveal that schools in the North West have been more successful in tackling bullying than elsewhere. Just under two-thirds of pupils (62 per cent) said they had never been bullied while nearly three-quarters (73 per cent) believe their teachers are aware of the issue.

However, bullying appears to be more widespread in the Midlands as 43 per cent of pupils reveal that they have been victims. Pupils in Wales are the most likely to receive threats of violence as 31 per cent said this had happened to them in the preceding twelve months. The South West witnessed slightly more actual attacks as 16 per cent of pupils reported incidents.

Commenting on the survey, Peter Smith, general secretary of ATL, said: 'Schools do attempt to provide young people with a safe environment to learn. However, no matter how much a school tries to change its culture, bullying has a tendency to rear its ugly head. It seems that youngsters are now increasingly becoming victims of violence.

'These findings are shocking. If young people are worried about their personal safety while at school, this begs the question, how are they going to feel once they are in the big wide world?'.

For further information, please contact: Association of Teachers and Lecturers (ATL). Tel: 020-7930 6441. Fax: 020-7930 1359. E-mail: info@atl.org.uk Web site: www.askatl.org.uk

• The ATL survey was conducted by Market and Opinion Research International (MORI) between 17 January and 29 February 2000. 115 middle and secondary schools in England and Wales participated and 2,610 pupils returned questionnaires.

© Market & Opinion Research International (MORI)

Schoolbully.com

Cutting-edge technology is making some pupils' lives a misery

By Amy Cox

Christopher Fletcher was amazed when he came down to breakfast one morning to find his 14-year-old son Mark in floods of tears, begging not to be sent to school that day. His amazement turned to shock and rage when he found out that some of his son's classmates had set up a web page devoted to Mark. Posted on the site was a variety of abuse and taunts. It had already been seen not only by the pupils in Mark's class, some of whom had accessed it via the computers at their school, but by other children in the area, one of whom had phoned to alert Mark.

Christopher already knew that there had been problems in Mark's class and that boys had been picking on each other throughout the year; but he had thought that the situation had been resolved. He was horrified to find that the extremely public humiliation via techno-bullying was the culmination of a sustained campaign directed against his son.

'The internet may be a wonderful thing, but this was just evil; it wasn't a game, it wasn't schoolboy banter, it was a very nasty, public, personal attack,' he says. 'The page said he was fat, gay, had no friends – and plenty more like that. The site had been accessed via the school computers during the lunch-hours, it had been seen by most of his class, by his peer group, and he was extremely upset.'

The site has been taken down now, as far as Christopher knows; but the damage has been done. 'It's very worrying, because there's no control at all over what goes up on the web.'

It is the first case of this particular kind of techno-bullying that Hereward Harrison, director of policy at ChildLine, has come across;

but, sadly, he's not surprised. 'Young people are very inventive,' he says. 'We have heard of instances of using text messages on mobile phones to bully other children. The technology for this kind of behaviour is there now, and bullies are turning it to their own ends.'

Similarly, Susan Littlemore, communications director at Parentline Plus, a charity that runs a free help and information service on all aspects of parenting, is concerned but hardly amazed at the emergence of techno-bullying. 'Kids are very ingenious in the ways that they bully each other. Technology is moving on and children today are extremely computer-literate; I should think that any technological framework that's set up to stop children saying horrible things online will quickly be circumvented.'

So what can be done to help children who find themselves in a similar situation to Mark Fletcher? Hereward Harrison says that dealing with techno-bullying starts with gathering evidence and getting adult help. The first step he recommends is to keep a detailed diary of what's happening, including any abusive emails or downloaded web pages, and show it to a parent or teacher. 'Making the situation public is very positive when it comes to bullying. Then you need to set up a meeting between parents, school and the young person themselves, and formulate a plan of action; if necessary go to school governors, or the local education authority. In some cases the intervention of the police has been very effective.'

But when Christopher Fletcher approached his son's school, he found that getting help was not easy. 'They first said that because the site hadn't been concocted on school equipment, it was nothing to do with them. When I pointed out that it had been accessed from school computers, they were more interested. I had a letter from the head saying he had spoken to the boys concerned, but the overall tone was one of "boys will be boys".'

Fletcher was sufficiently incensed by this cavalier approach to seek legal advice. 'What the school took some time to appreciate was that Mark has been libelled. It's like putting up a sign on a roundabout that everyone can read. We're entitled to sue for libel on his behalf. I am going to tell the school that if it happens again, we will be suing – taking out injunctions against the parents of the boys concerned, impounding their home computers, and, if school computers were used, impounding those too.'

Christopher Fletcher may not be so far off the mark in thinking about the legal implications of techno-bullying. In April of this year, a professor at the City College in San Francisco launched a libel lawsuit over allegations made by students on a website that he is 'racist and mentally ill'. Daniel Curzon Brown describes the site as 'evil' and claims that the attacks had made him 'depressed and afraid'. He is currently suing the company that runs the website.

According to Susan Littlemore, schools don't always do all they can to help bullied children in more conventional situations, let alone ones aggravated by the use of technology. She says that many parents are let down by teachers, even when their child has been

bullied to the end of his or her tether. 'Parents are often surprised by how long their child has managed to conceal the issue, and when the parents find out, it's often an extreme situation by then. Not only is the child disturbed, but the parents are extremely distressed.'

When it comes to techno-bullying, says Littlemore, 'the argument isn't about creating a sterile environment where abuses can't happen, because that's probably impossible'. The way forward, she says, is for schools to set up an anti-bullying policy. 'We are finding this isn't happening. Parents with legitimate concerns who approach their child's school aren't being heard. Getting parents involved is essential. It's easy for those who are delivering education to focus solely on education, which is why parents need to become involved and voice their concerns.'

Teachers, however, would argue that they are beleaguered enough already without adding to their workload. 'It's impossible for teachers to police what's happening outside

---

'Kids are very ingenious in the ways that they bully each other. Technology is moving on and children today are extremely computer-literate'

---

school – it's difficult enough inside,' says a spokeswoman for the National Union of Teachers. 'If the teachers are aware of bullying, they can do something about it, but bullied children are often very secretive. Teachers can't see what children are doing on their computers at home; they can't monitor pupils' private lives. That is where parents come in.'

She recommends keeping home computers in shared spaces. 'If the computer is in the living room then you can see on a regular basis as you pass by what your child is doing.' The computer shouldn't be hidden away in the child's bedroom, she says. 'If the parents of the children involved in this particular case had known what their children were doing, they might have been able to put a stop to it. Parents must monitor home use.'

Littlemore isn't so sure. 'Whenever a community is set up, that community has responsibilities. Schools need to take that on board. When schools say they don't know what to do about bullying or it's not up to them to deal with it, the parents are stuck in the middle – it's very unpleasant.'

• Parentline Plus has an anti-bullying initiative for parents; for more information call their free helpline on 0808 800 2222 (textline 0800 783 6783) or visit www.parentlineplus.org.uk

• First appeared in *The Guardian*, Spetember 2000.

© Amy Cox

One-third of children are 'bullying' victims

**By Tony Halpin,
Education Correspondent**

The disturbing extent of school bullying was revealed yesterday in a survey suggesting one in three children had been victimised in the past year.

In many cases, teachers were unaware there was a problem, despite the fact that nearly one in ten pupils had stayed away from classes in fear.

Of 2,600 children questioned, a quarter said they had been threatened with violence by other children and one in seven said they had been assaulted.

The problem was most serious among younger pupils who were twice as likely to suffer as teenagers.

More than half of 11-year-olds said they had been bullied compared to a quarter of 15-and 16-year-olds.

Older pupils were more likely to report that teachers were ignorant of bullying, with 41 per cent claiming staff were unaware of problems. Overall, 30 per cent thought teachers failed to pay enough attention to bullying.

One in four pupils said they feared for their safety on the journey to and from school each day. Girls were particularly worried, with 30 per cent saying they had concerns compared to 22 per cent of boys.

Girls were also more afraid of violence, although boys were three times more likely to be threatened. Boys were also three times more likely to be physically attacked, with 19 per cent reporting that they had been assaulted.

The survey of pupils in middle and secondary schools also found regional variations. Bullying was worst in the Midlands, where 43 per cent of children said they had been victims. Pupils in Wales were most likely to have been threatened (31 per cent) and children in the South West were the most likely to suffer assault (16 per cent).

Schools in the North West appeared to be most successful at tackling the problem. Just under two-thirds of children said they had never suffered from bullying and nearly three-quarters believed their teachers were aware of the need to deal with the issue.

> **Older pupils were more likely to report that teachers were ignorant of bullying, with 41 per cent claiming staff were unaware of problems**

Members of the Association of Teachers and Lecturers, which commissioned the survey, said that Government pressure on schools to reduce expulsions was undermining attempts to maintain classroom discipline.

More than £500million is being spent in extra support for schools, designed to help them deal with difficult children.

But in a motion to be debated at the union's annual conference, which starts in Belfast today, delegates are due to warn the Government that 'its enthusiasm for inclusion must not do a disservice to any children in mainstream schools'.

General secretary Peter Smith said: 'It seems that youngsters are now increasingly becoming victims of violence.'

But Margaret Morrissey, of the National Confederation of Parent-Teacher Associations, said all schools were now required to draw up anti-bullying policies.

Their success in making pupils aware of the harm caused by hurtful remarks may have had a bearing on the survey's results, as many children now classed this as bullying and were more likely to report it as such, she added.

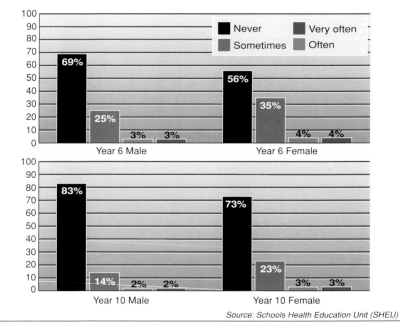

Fear of being bullied

Students were asked: 'Do you ever feel afraid of going to school because of bullying?' The females are more fearful than the males, and the Year 6s are more concerned than the Year 10s.

Source: Schools Health Education Unit (SHEU)

Blair backs teenager's cyberwar on bullies

Website launched by pupil to help fellow victims is an instant hit

Tony Blair has written to a bullied teenager to praise the Internet site he has set up to help other victims.

Oliver Watts, 15, designed and launched pupiline.com last month and has already received 155,000 'hits' or web visits from other children.

The Prime Minister told him: 'I was sorry to read you were bullied.

'I welcome initiatives such as yours to help children who are bullied and am pleased you are exploiting new technology.

'I am pleased to endorse pupiline.com. I am also pleased that something positive has come out of your experiences.'

He added in his letter that the Department of Education is following suit and plans to launch an anti-bullying website. The project will be part of an initiative next term which will also include updated anti-bullying packs for schools and a video for pupils.

Oliver said: 'I am so excited the Prime Minister has backed my site. I feel like I've got through to the top man and the Government is not just turning a blind eye.

'I hope Tony Blair lives up to his word and really does something that will make a difference.'

The teenager, who attends the Gilberd School, Colchester, Essex, set up the site after his life was made hell at a previous school.

'No one was my friend,' he said. 'It was me against the other 150 kids in my year. It was mostly name-calling, humiliations in lessons, verbal abuse. I was beaten up a couple of times, but verbal bullying can hurt more than you think. I would dread walking into class, wondering what would happen next. I felt terrible.'

After he began feigning illness to avoid class, his parents, who are both teachers, moved him to his present school. His father David said:

'We are proud of how he turned an experience that could have set him back into a force for good. We also think this may be the first website to receive official backing from the Prime Minister.'

Mr Watts said his son was so buoyed up by the support he is featuring other issues on pupiline, such as exam stress and careers.

This week Oliver, who has a younger brother Harry, appeared live on US television and he has also been on *Kilroy*.

---

pupiline.net

Information from pupiline.net

Unfortunately bullying is very common in schools and in places of work everywhere. Most people think of bullying as physical – hitting, punching, kicking, and stealing; but bullying is anything that makes a person do something they do not want to do, name calling etc. The main problem is that too many people and too many schools stand by and let it happen.

You as a pupil have certain rights, your school must do certain things to protect you from bullying. The following information came from the DFEE (Department for Education and Employment) – these guys are responsible for writing the laws that tell teachers and schools how to work. Their website is at www.dfee.gov.uk:

'Each school should have a clear school behaviour policy. It should make clear the boundaries of what is acceptable, the hierarchy of sanctions, arrangements for their consistent and fair application, and a linked system of rewards for good behaviour. It should promote respect for others, intolerance of bullying and harassment, the importance of self-discipline and the difference between "right" and "wrong".'

What to do:
- Remember you don't deserve to be bullied, it's the bullies' problem!
- Talk about it to someone who will listen
- Tell a teacher you trust
- Stick to facts and bring a witness
- Defend yourself if necessary
- Stay in a group
- Be firm, if they pressure you shout 'NO'; it'll get attention

What not to do:
- Do not ignore the bullying – make a noise about it
- Don't confront the bully
- Don't fight back except to defend yourself – it only makes it worse believe me!
- Don't get in a slanging match
- If you are scared or intimidated get away and get help
- Don't fight to keep your stuff – you are more important!

• The above information is from the Pupiline website which can be found at www.pupiline.net

'The website has helped me a lot but above all, it's given me a chance to help,' he said. 'There must be thousands going through what I've been through. I want them to know they're not alone.'

He receives hundreds of messages from pupils taunted by bullies. 'The website really seems to be helping. Last week a girl posted a message saying she had taken an overdose and nearly died because she couldn't cope,' said Oliver.

'I wrote back offering advice and so did other people who saw the message. She replied saying that she knew she was no longer alone.'

Last week two headteachers' associations also endorsed pupiline as a new report showed that a third of pupils suffer bullying.

• The Pupiline web site can be found at www.pupiline.net

Every week, 2,300 children become classroom victims

By Walter Ellis

Tomorrow, as every weekday, some 2,338 of the nation's 3.8 million secondary school pupils can expect to be bullied. Some of them will only be teased. It may be their names, it may be the way they look, it may be the colour of their skin that provokes the taunts. Others will have their hair pulled or their legs kicked or their eyes blacked. A few may be more seriously hurt.

Most of those who are bullied once will be bullied again – some of them relentlessly. It will make their lives a misery. One or two each year may even attempt to kill themselves to escape the misery that starts as soon as they leave home and begin the long walk to the 'best days of their lives'.

In the time of *Tom Brown's Schooldays*, it was considered normal, or at least usual, for older, stronger boys to tease and torture their younger, weaker brethren. The point of Dr Arnold's intervention in the case of the egregious Flashman was that he, the headmaster, re-presented a new, humane approach, which would no longer tolerate Flashman's everyday excesses.

Similarly, in *Nicholas Nickleby*, Nicholas's assault on Squeers for flogging his charges in Dotheboys Hall represents Dickens's passionately held conviction that something had to be done to reduce the acceptance of barbarity in England's schools.

Today, a century and a half on, the impulse to bully remains little altered. Football hooliganism, a group extension of the genre, shows the level to which violent behaviour can descend. All that has changed is society's attitude and, with it, the rules of the game.

'Bullying,' said the Education Secretary David Blunkett soon after taking office in 1997, 'can leave an indelible scar. The emotional and mental distress it causes can damage a child's education. It can lead to disaffection and truancy, blighting a young person's future life.'

Mr Blunkett continued: 'I want all schools to treat bullying very seriously and deal with it promptly and firmly whenever and wherever it occurs. To do that, all schools must have an effective whole-school policy to which all staff, pupils and parents are committed and have played a part in developing.'

According to a study carried out by Goldsmith's College, London, the number of pupils who claimed they had been bullied fell by 72,000 over the past 10 years, to an annual total of 456,000 – 12 per cent of the secondary total. At the same time, the number of bullies fell from 560,000 to 240,000.

At the beginning of this year, Professor Peter Smith, a psychologist, said that there had been a 'sea change' in the way that the issue of bullying was tackled, and the UK was no longer Europe's worst offender in the field.

Parents whose personal experience runs counter to DoE propaganda may feel that all that has happened is that bullying is being wished out of existence and that the issue has been swept under a carpet of statistics. As Professor Smith warned: 'We must not be complacent. There is a lot of work still to be done.'

Beating the bully

It causes misery, it wrecks lives, it can even lead to suicide. Jerome Monahan on the horror of bullying.

Thousands of children in Britain are suffering the misery of being bullied. Between 1998 and 1999 the national charity ChildLine received 22,332 calls from children who were being picked on. Many put up with the torture, but some find it too awful to bear. Between 10 and 14 cases of childhood suicide occur every year as a direct result of bullying.

What is bullying?

Most bullying means repeated acts of intimidation. It is deliberately carried out. It happens when a person or a group tries to dominate others whom they consider weaker. It always causes the victims pain. The charity Kidscape says bullying can be physical, verbal, emotional, racist or sexual.

Does it always include violence?

No. A recent survey of 2,300 six- to nine-year-olds found the most common bullying was name-calling.

Who are the bullies?

Bullies are usually people with problems themselves. They may feel inadequate or scared and use bullying as a cover. The consequences for bullies who receive no help can be serious. According to research conducted by Professor Dan Olweus, children who bully are four times as likely to become young offenders with criminal records when they leave school. Over the past 15 years bullying by girls has increased. Many reasons for this have been suggested, including even the way some styles of behaviour are promoted by pop groups.

Who are the bullied?

Bullies are quick to spot characteristics that might mark someone as being different from the crowd. How the victim behaves is crucial. If the bully gets away with the first act, he or she is likely to continue.

Is being violent back the answer?

There is no guarantee that meeting violence with violence will solve anything. It may result in the victim being excluded from school or even seriously injured.

What are the first things that someone being bullied should do?

Tell an adult. No one deserves to be bullied and speaking about it should not make the situation worse. In a recent survey, seven out of eight victims of bullying felt that speaking out made things better.

What protection do pupils have a right to expect while at school?

Schools have a 'duty of care' for pupils. This means they must do all they can to protect students from harm. Since September 1999, the law requires schools to draw up an anti-bullying policy.

What should schools do to solve the problem of bullying?

The best thing is to stop bullying before it starts. Pupils need to discuss the subject and know how to seek help. Young people need to be taught how to solve conflicts without being aggressive. In some schools students are trained to be 'peer mediators' – stepping in to support fellow pupils in difficulties.

Over the past 15 years bullying by girls has increased. Many reasons for this have been suggested, including even the way some styles of behaviour are promoted by pop groups

---

Is bullying against the law?

If a bully hurts someone physically, they are guilty of assault. The age at which a person in England is considered to be capable of responsibility for a criminal act has recently been reduced to 10. In Scotland, it is eight. There are also laws that protect people from harassment.

What are the most common false ideas about bullying?

'I was bullied at school and it didn't do me any harm.' 'You need to learn how to stand up for yourself.' 'Sticks and stones may break your bones but names can never hurt you.'

Myths like these are unhelpful because they give some adults an excuse not to take the matter seriously and make victims feel that they should put up with bullying.

Why is bullying such a serious matter?

Anything that can cause young people to kill themselves must be taken seriously. For those who suffer in silence, the effects of bullying can affect the rest of their lives.

A survey by Kidscape in 1998 among 1,000 adults showed that many felt their school days had been stolen from them by bullies and that they had been haunted by feelings of anxiety and bitterness ever since. One 34-year-old woman told the researchers: 'If I had enjoyed school I might have bloomed into a more confident person. It makes me feel I have wasted my life being too careful and nervous to succeed.'

- Kidscape 020 7730 3300
- ChildLine 0800 1111
- ChildLine Scotland has a dedicated bullying line 0800 441111
- Anti-Bullying Campaign 0207 378 1446

• First appeared in *The Guardian*, March 2000.

© *Jerome Monahan*

Stop bullies or pay price, schools told

By Tony Halpin, Education Correspondent

Schools were warned yesterday that they will have to expel classroom bullies more quickly or face costly claims for compensation under the new Human Rights Act.

Head teachers' leader David Hart said failure to deal with bullies could expose schools to claims from parents of victims that their children were being subjected to 'inhuman and degrading treatment'.

Claims would be lodged under Article Three of the European Convention on Human Rights, which the Act incorporates into English law from October.

'If people make successful claims the cost could easily exceed a million pounds in the first year unless heads are given the appropriate flexibility to exclude pupils permanently in the event of inhuman or degrading treatment,' added Mr Hart, who is general secretary of the National Association of Head Teachers.

He called on the Government to rewrite guidance on expulsions issued only last week to make clear that school should expel pupils for bullying or racial and sexual harassment.

The association sent out legal advice to its 32,000 members yesterday, warning that the rights of other children could be infringed if appeals panels overturn expulsions and order heads to accept bullies back into their schools.

'To suffer violence or bullying is, in principle, to suffer degrading treatment,' the advice said. 'Heads may well have a duty to take action to prevent a violation of human rights by protecting individuals from violence or bullying.

'Accordingly, there is a positive duty on a head to exclude a pupil if that pupil's continued attendance at the school was likely to result in some other identifiable individual being subjected to degrading treatment.'

Mr Hart said schools, local education authorities and appeals panels had to recognise that the Act conferred new rights on pupils and parents in an 'increasingly litigious society'.

He went on: 'The number of suicides and other tragedies suffered as a result of alleged bullying mean schools have to be on the alert for the implications of the Human Rights Act.'

While the NAHT is urging heads to act more swiftly against unruly pupils, some legal experts believe schools could also face demands for compensation under the same legislation from parents who claim their children have been wrongly expelled.

They point to a separate safeguard in the Convention on Human Rights which states: 'No person shall be denied the right to education.'

That is intended to protect the right of religious groups and minorities to educate their children in line with their own 'philosophical convictions'.

But lawyers believe the extent to which this might apply to children expelled from school will have to be tested in the courts.

Mr Hart said he would be seeking talks with Education Secretary David Blunkett next week to try to persuade him to include bullying and racial and sexual harassment in a list of offences for which children should be expelled.

'Heads may well have a duty to take action to prevent a violation of human rights'

The Government told appeals panels in its revised guidance issued last week not to overrule heads where expulsions related to 'serious actual or threatened violence', sexual abuse, the sale of illegal drugs, or 'persistent and malicious disruptive behaviour'.

Schools should also be supported where a pupil had been expelled 'in line with an explicit discipline policy'.

Schools Minister Jacqui Smith told a teachers' conference that she believed this covered pupils who 'persistently flout school rules with respect to vandalism, racial harassment, or bullying'. But Mr Hart said heads wanted this spelt out clearly.

If parents appealed successfully to have their children reinstated, heads would be forced to teach him or her in isolation in an effort to protect their schools from claims under the Human Rights Act.

Mr Blunkett sent out guidance last September as part of a drive to cut expulsions by a third by 2002.

It was changed last week after heads complained that discipline was being undermined because appeals panels were returning unruly children to schools under pressure from LEAs desperate to meet expulsions targets.

A spokesman for Mr Blunkett insisted the NAHT's concerns were already covered by the guidance. But the union's warning echoed points raised on Monday by Cherie Booth QC, the Prime Minister's wife, who is an expert on human rights law.

She said the Act imposed a duty on public authorities to prevent abuses from occurring, although she expected the courts to be 'sensible and discourage the opening of the floodgates'.

The Department for Education and Employment said it was confident the advice met the requirements of the Human Rights Act.

© The Daily Mail, 2000

Take action against bullying

Information from Bully B'ware

The United Nations Charter of Rights for Children states, in part, that:

- every child has the right to an education; and
- every child has the right to be safe.

As adults working in the public education system, it is our duty to provide a safe school environment for all students. The following qualities are essential for a healthy and safe school environment.

Safe schools:

1. Are free from violence
2. Are nurturing, caring and respectful of everyone
3. Are physically and psychologically healthy
4. Promote sensible risk taking
5. Enhance the self-esteem of all.

Bullying has no place in a safe school.

'Take Action Against Bullying' was written to educate students, parents, teachers and administrators. We believe that by taking action against bullying, we can make a significant difference to the lives of all students, and have a profoundly positive impact on the climate of your school.

What is bullying?

Bullying in its truest form is comprised of a series of repeated intentionally cruel incidents, involving the same children, in the same bully and victim roles. This, however, does not mean that in order for bullying to occur there must be repeat offences. Bullying can consist of a single interaction. Bullying behaviour may also be defined as a criminal act if the bully is twelve years of age or older.

Common characteristics of bullying

So, what makes a bullying incident? Certain conditions must exist for a bullying incident to occur. Lots of kids joke around with each other,

call each other names, or engage in some fairly physical horse-play and yet these incidents are not deemed as bullying when they occur between certain children. The difference lies in the relationship of the bully and victim, and in the intent of the interaction.

Bullying usually, although not always, occurs between individuals who are not friends. In a bullying situation, there is a power difference between the bully and the victim. For instance, the bully may be bigger, tougher, physically stronger or be able to intimidate others or have the power to exclude others from their social group.

The intention of bullying is to put the victim in distress in some way. Bullies seek power.

Bullying knows no financial, cultural or social bounds. Bullying may not look exactly the same everywhere, but it has the same devastating effect on everyone, and during adolescence, bullying is not a problem that usually sorts itself out.

The effects of bullying last a lifetime. It causes misery for the bully's victims, and leaves a lasting impression on all those who witness repeated bullying incidents.

Kinds of bullies

Physical bullies

Physical bullies are action-oriented. This type of bullying includes hitting or kicking the victim, or taking or damaging the victim's property. This is the least sophisticated type of bullying because it is so easy to identify. Physical bullies are soon known to the entire population in the school. As they get older, their attacks usually become more aggressive. These aggressive characteristics manifest themselves as bullies become adults.

Verbal bullies

Verbal bullies use words to hurt or humiliate another person. Verbal bullying includes name-calling, insulting, making racist comments and constant teasing. This type of bullying is the easiest to inflict on other children. It is quick and to the point. It can occur in the least amount of time available, and its effects can be more devastating in some ways than physical bullying because there are no visible scars.

Relational bullies

Relational or relationship bullies try to convince their peers to exclude or

reject a certain person or people and cut the victims off from their social connections. This type of bullying is linked to verbal bullying and usually occurs when children (most often girls) spread nasty rumours about others or exclude an ex-friend from the peer group. The most devastating effect with this type of bullying is the rejection by the peer group at a time when children most need their social connections.

Reactive victims

Reactive victims straddle a fence of being a bully and/or victim. They are often the most difficult to identify because at first glance they seem to be targets for other bullies. However, reactive victims often taunt bullies, and bully other people themselves. Most of the incidents are physical in nature. These victims are impulsive and react quickly to intentional and unintentional physical encounters. In some cases, reactive victims begin as victims and become bullies as they try to retaliate. A reactive victim will approach a person who has been bullying him/her and say something like, 'You better not bug me today, otherwise I'll tell the teacher and boy, will you be in trouble, so you just better watch out.'

Statements such as this are akin to waving a red flag in front of a raging bull, and may provoke a bully into action. Reactive victims then fight back and claim self-defence. Reactive victims need to learn how to avoid bullies.

What makes a bully?

Bullying behaviour can be identified as early as pre-school age, and some children who are bullies continue this behaviour into adulthood. Most children learn to control their anger and fighting instincts as they grow older, but not the bully. These children have special characteristics. Children who systematically bully others usually have a group of children they bully regularly while other bullies randomly target a variety of students.

Bullies have particular behaviour and personality traits. Dr. Sam Samenow describes these as:

- greater than average aggressive behaviour patterns

- the desire to dominate peers
- the need to feel in control, to win
- no sense of remorse for hurting another child
- a refusal to accept responsibility for his/her behaviour.

Parent(s) of bullies usually support their child's aggressive behaviour toward other children and often bully their child.

What makes a victim?

Why aren't all children victims? Research on bullying states that sixty per cent of all students are never involved in any kind of bullying incidents, either as victims or as bullies (*Psychology Today*, Sept. 1996). However, every day in schools, many students witness bullying incidents as they happen, and this forces their involvement. Often, these students do not realise that what they are witnessing is, in fact, bullying. Good-natured teasing and rough-housing are only fun if both parties involved agree that it is fun. The power difference between bullies and victims determines the nature of the interaction.

Most children are approached by a bully early in their school career, and/or when they change schools. It is often the child's reaction to that first encounter with being bullied which determines whether or not he/she will be approached again. Children who are victimised tend to display 'vulnerable behaviours'. People who are identified as being highly vulnerable are often singled out as victims.

What happens to bullies?

The lifelong outlook for bullies is not good. If bullies don't learn how to change their behaviour, the pattern of bullying behaviour often becomes a habit as the bully gets older.

Bullies have average social popularity up to approximately age 14 or 15. In fact, some children even look up to bullies in some ways because they are powerful and do what they want to, or have to, to get their way with their peers. However, by late adolescence, the bully's popularity begins to wane. By senior high school, if a bully is still attending school, his or her peer group includes other bullies, or more seriously, he or she has developed or is developing gang alliances. By late high school, schoolyard bullying is a rare occurrence, but what takes its place is more serious.

By age 24, up to sixty per cent of people who are identified as childhood bullies have at least one criminal conviction. A study spanning 35 years by psychologist E. Eron at the University of Michigan found that children who were named by their school mates, at age eight, as the bullies of the school were often bullies throughout their lives. In this longitudinal study of bullies, many of these children, as adults, required more support from government agencies. For example, these children later had more court convictions, more alcoholism, more antisocial personality disorders and used more of the mental health services than the other children.

Unless new behaviours are learned and adopted, bullies continue to bully throughout their lifetime. They bully their mates, their children, and possibly their underlings in their place of business. Bullying gets them what they want, and although some bullies learn to refine the art of bullying in their professional lives and use it in situations where there is a power imbalance, it creates less than harmonious relations in the workplace.

What happens to victims?

Adults, like children, resent being bullied, except that adult victims have more options available to them than do child victims. Children cannot escape the schoolyard, the changing room, or the cafeteria. Sometimes, victims do not survive the torture and humiliation of bullying.

In most situations, victims do survive, but carry their emotional scars for a lifetime.

By senior high school, regular bullying incidents are often a thing of the past, but all victims know who the bullies are, and avoid them. By age 16 or 17, bullies and victims are usually moving in different directions in terms of curricular interests in school, therefore their paths rarely cross. Social groupings are clearly defined by this time in a student's life and invisible boundaries have been drawn.

When a child has been repeatedly victimised, certain behaviours and attitudes tend to emerge which are inconsistent with his/her typical behaviours. Often children are too embarrassed and humiliated to report victimisation.

Reasons why we must take action against bullying:

- by age 24, 60% of identified bullies have a criminal conviction
- children who are repeatedly victimised sometimes see suicide as their only escape
- bullying is one of the most underrated and enduring problems in schools today
- schools are a prime location for bullying
- bullies lose their popularity as they get older and are eventually disliked by the majority of students
- primary age children who were labelled by their peers as bullies required more support as adults from government agencies, had more court convictions, more alcoholism, more antisocial personality disorders and used more mental health services
- many adults do not know how to intervene in bullying situations, therefore bullying is often overlooked
- bullying occurs once every seven minutes
- on average, bullying episodes are brief, approximately 37 seconds long

- the emotional scars from bullying can last a lifetime
- the majority of bullying occurs in or close to school buildings
- most victims are unlikely to report bullying
- only 25% of students report that teachers intervene in bullying situations, while 71% of teachers believe they always intervene.

We believe that bullying can be significantly reduced in schools if teachers, support staff, parent groups, student councils and administrators join together to take action against bullying.

Benefits of an anti-bullying policy

In talking to parents over the past years, it is clear that what they want most for their children is to know that they are safe at school. When a child does not feel safe at school, it affects everything else that goes on in that child's life. Many schools have an unofficial reputation for tolerating bullying. This reputation is usually common knowledge throughout the student community. In these schools more children tend to feel anxious about their personal safety and as a result many are reluctant to attend. By the time a school has a public reputation for being a 'tough school', many victims have suffered in silence.

Once the issue of bullying is brought into the open by the school, and the community is made aware of the 'No Bullying' policy, the school gains a reputation of being safe for all

children and is seen as an active partner in taking care of children.

The benefits to students are significant as well. When children know that the school they attend actively works to make the learning environment a safe environment, and that bullying is not tolerated, they can afford to relax their guard and divert more of their attention to learning rather than staying safe. Even students who cannot be categorised as victims or bullies, but who witness bullying, feel more comfortable when they know that the school community, students, staff and administration stand together against bullying.

Regardless of what kind of school environment students have previously encountered, when they enter a school with a Zero Tolerance for bullying, students who have bullying potential usually test the policy. For this reason, it is important that the school maintains the active teaching of non-bullying behaviours, and publishes school-based bullying statistics. Students need to know that this is not just a 'shot in the dark', and that the policy will be reviewed and maintained each and every year.

Although it is best to have the entire school working toward a reduction in the number of bullying incidents, in situations where this cannot be achieved, classroom teachers can adopt individual programmes. This is not as desirable for obvious reasons, but it is a start to tackling the bullying problem.

What schools can do

A major cause of stress at school for children is the fear of being taunted or bullied. Kids who are bullied are two to three times more likely to have headaches or other illnesses.

Schools need to establish a social climate where physical aggression and bullying are not used to gain popularity, maintain group leadership or influence others to do what they are told to do. No one deserves to be bullied. Once the 60% of children who are neither victims nor bullies adopt the attitude that bullying is an unacceptable behaviour, schools are well on their way to having a successful bullying programme.

Schools need to advertise the fact that they have adopted a Zero Tolerance policy for bullying, and that they have a working Anti-Bullying plan in force. School faculty must maintain a high profile in terms of the behavioural expectations of their students in order to gain support from the community and send a clear message to the families of present and future students that bullying will not be tolerated.

Once a school has established itself as a safe place for all students, school personnel will need to continually work at maintaining that reputation. It is a difficult task that requires the school faculty to put student safety at the top of their priority list. Remember, students who do not feel safe at school are unlikely to perform as well academically as they are capable, thus possibly impeding their future opportunities. A commitment by the staff to no bullying in the school must be a long-term undertaking. When a new school year begins, staff should be sure Anti-Bullying policies have been included and discussed in the yearly goal-setting process.

Schools can create support groups where victims can concentrate on developing the skills needed to change their place within the social hierarchy of the student body. The goal is for the victim to become a part of the group of students who do not bully and are not bullied. Such change requires a great deal of time and effort, but it is possible, given the necessary support.

> *Schools need to advertise the fact that they have adopted a Zero Tolerance policy for bullying, and that they have a work-ing Anti-Bullying plan in force*

Students are key to a successful anti-bullying campaign

Students are key to a successful Anti-Bullying campaign primarily because they usually know who the bullies are long before the adults do.

When it comes to discipline or punishment issues, most students strongly believe in fairness and therefore welcome Anti-Bullying policies that encourage treating others with care and respect.

However, students are more likely to support an Anti-Bullying campaign when they have been directly involved in determining the need for such a programme, and deciding on its implementation. This includes developing Anti-Bullying policies and subsequent school-wide or classroom activities. It is necessary for students to promote the concept that caring for others is a valued quality, one that they accept and encourage.

Teachers need to be sensitive to the fact that the level of student participation in the Anti-Bullying campaign will vary. Once students are mobilised to take action against bullies, they must feel secure that teachers understand their need to stay safe. For some students this means ensuring that the information

Brothers, sisters and friends

Brothers, sisters and friends often know that someone is being bullied long before teachers and parents do.

What should they do? Sometimes the person being bullied asks them not to do anything. Sometimes they do nothing in case the bullies start to pick on them.

But doing nothing usually means that the bullying carries on, or that the bullies become more confident and choose more victims. Part of the fun that bullies get comes from the reaction of bystanders. If you do nothing the bullies may think that you approve of what they are doing.

Here are some things you can do. If any of them do not work, don't give up. Try something else.

- Persuade the person being bullied to talk to an adult – this may be a teacher or a parent.
- Encourage the person being bullied to talk to you about what is happening.
- Offer to speak to an adult on the bullied person's behalf.
- Let the bullies know that you are not so frightened of them that you will do nothing and that you are determined to see that they stop.
- Raise the issue of bullying with the student council (if the school has one) or in discussions in subjects like English, drama, religious education, or social education.
- Involve as many people as possible. In particular try to make sure that teachers know what is going on – but, most of all, talk to somebody.

Here are some things you should not do

- Do not use violence against the bullies – you may end up being accused of being a bully yourself.
- Do not tell the person being bullied to deal with the problem on their own – if they could they wouldn't have asked you for help.
- Do not try to deal with things on your own

© The Scottish Council for Research in Education (SCRE)

they share will not cause them to lose status in their peer group. Confidentiality must be maintained in order for the programme to be viewed by the students as credible. As well, to help students actively participate and take on the challenge of reducing bullying, it is very important that they learn the difference between 'ratting' and 'reporting'. 'Ratting' occurs when a student tells about an inappropriate act with the idea of getting another student into trouble with the administration. 'Reporting' happens when a student tells to protect the safety of another student. Once students have an understanding of the difference between the two, reporting bullying incidents becomes much less of a social taboo.

Thanks for your interest in this important issue.

Bully B'ware Productions has a book, video and posters to help students, parents, teachers and administrators 'Take Action Against Bullying'.

Bully B'ware Productions, 1421 King Albert Avenue, Coquitlam, British Columbia, Canada V3J 1Y3 (604) 936-8000.

• The above is an extract from Bully B'ware's web site which can be found at www.bullybeware.com

© *Bully B'ware*

Standing up to bullies

Headteachers do have the power to exclude the most disruptive pupils and teachers are being offered more help to tackle bullying before it gets out of hand. Two schools reveal the steps they have taken.

Jack's story

Jack, a ten-year-old pupil at a medium-sized primary school, was kicked by a gang of three older pupils outside the school gates. It was just another in a long line of incidents in a school which had, what the head described, as a 'culture of bullying'. A few days later Matthew and Sam, both aged nine, complained of persistent verbal abuse from classmates. A survey found that almost half the pupils had been bullied, while a quarter said they had bullied others.

The head decided it had to stop. After a special staff meeting, a formal whole-school anti-bullying policy was drafted and all pupils, staff and parents were invited to comment.

Jack was pleased to see copies posted in every classroom and Matthew even felt able to take part in the discussion of bullying that his teacher started in class. For Matthew and Sam, the school's new active approach made a huge difference; the name-calling has almost entirely stopped and both feel better prepared to cope with future incidents.

Lunchtime supervisors also attended a one-day training course on bullying.

The more pro-active stance they were encouraged to take has helped to change the atmosphere. 'I no longer let the children hide behind the excuse that they were only playing,' one says. Jack also hasn't experienced any further violence and research has shown physical bullying incidents reported at the school have fallen by 41 per cent.

Rashida's story

Rashida had a tough time settling in when she joined a city comprehensive at the age of 14. One boy kept up a subtle stream of racist abuse and she found it hard to make friends. She also kept being left out of the other girls' games. The girls had whispered and started rumours about her. Her parents read the school's code of conduct and equal opportunities policy and encouraged Rashida to contact the peer support system.

Rashida talked to a Year Eight pupil who'd been trained as a peer supporter and got helpful advice on how to respond to the bullies. 'Rather than ignoring the problem and pretending it wasn't there, I could respond assertively to the cold-shouldering,' she says. 'I was able to penetrate the social circle and be accepted.'

Rashida's case was discussed at the weekly peer supporters' half-hour lunchtime supervision sessions, where ideas on how to respond were aired. Rashida took their advice and stood up for herself.

She also encouraged other ethnic minority pupils to report the

bully when he directed racist comments at them. Between 1998 and 1999 the peer support scheme has encouraged more pupils to report bullying and the numbers who said they had been bullied fell from 53 per cent to 42 per cent.

Top tips for a bully-free school

- David Blunkett wrote to schools in January to make it clear that heads can exclude violent pupils.
- Appeal panels should not normally reinstate a pupil who has been permanently excluded for serious actual or threatened violence against another pupil or member of staff.
- Establish a whole-school policy, involving pupils, parents and staff. A written document sets out the school's aims and the strategies to be followed.
- Get senior management to take a lead, and make sure all teaching and non-teaching staff know what to do when bullying occurs.
- Get feedback from staff, parents, pupils and governors and hold regular surveys so that the policy can be regularly reviewed and updated.
- Give one teacher key responsibility for the policy.

• *Bullying: Don't Suffer in Silence* – an anti-bullying pack for schools will be published by the DfEE in the autumn. Names and details of pupils at these schools have been changed to protect their identities.

Preventing racist bullying

What schools can do. Information from Kidscape

No easy answers

In a school day crammed with demands, dealing with bullying, especially racist bullying, is one of the most difficult problems facing teachers. There are no easy answers or instant solutions, but the children's charity Kidscape has found the following suggestions to be effective.

Schools can ensure that:
- pupils are told from day one that bullying of any kind is not tolerated
- they carry out an anonymous survey of the pupils to find out if racist bullying is a problem and then act upon it
- parents are informed that the school is committed to ensuring racial harmony amongst its pupils, staff and the community
- they have materials, books, lessons and activities which are used in the curriculum to help the pupils learn appropriate ways to behave
- PSHE modules cover prejudice, direct/indirect discrimination, stereotypes, celebrating diversity
- their guidelines state that all pupils are entitled to feel safe and secure
- their ethos is one which values and respects people from all cultural, ethnic and religious backgrounds
- all staff and governors are trained

in equality issues, working with parents, supporting victims, changing negative behaviours and school procedures for resolving bullying.

Helping pupils

In order to support pupils, schools need to:
- work with staff and pupils together to create an anti-bullying policy that includes issues of racist bullying
- ensure that the policy is readily available to staff, parents and pupils. Some schools ask pupils to sign the policy and keep it in their school file
- explain that everyone has a part to play in preventing bullying –

no one is allowed to be a bystander. Anyone who knows about or witnesses bullying must tell and get help
- act when told about racist or any kind of bullying
- be aware and vigilant. If possible, the staff should try to uncover the bullying as this protects the victims from being seen as 'grassing' and further risking their safety
- provide a private way for frightened victims to tell, such as individual meetings with all pupils on a regular basis so no one is seen to be singled out or a box where children can anonymously post suggestions, complaints and comments

- ensure that the PSHE programme includes lessons in self-esteem and friendship skills, assertiveness, handling conflict
- teach all pupils bullying prevention programmes such as Kidscape which includes strategies such as:
  – ignore the bullying, pretend not to hear
  – walk away quickly; use body language to look determined, strong and positive even if you feel frightened inside
  – shout NO, GO AWAY as loudly as possible
  – always tell a trusted adult if you are bullied.

Consequences

Pupils, parents and staff need to know that racist bullying will not be tolerated and what will happen if it persists. It is important that schools:
- set up procedures for resolving incidents. A policy statement on its own is not enough – clear guidelines ensure action is taken
- ensure the safety and support of victims
- try first to mediate so that pupils are given a chance to resolve things peacefully, if possible
- realise that some pupils do not

> *Schools can ensure that pupils are told from day one that bullying of any kind is not tolerated*

appreciate the distress they are causing and are willing to change their behaviour
- help bullies to understand that their behaviour is completely unacceptable and that they must take responsibility for their actions, apologise and make amends
- use sanctions if initial attempts to stop the bullying fail
- record repeated and/or serious incidents of bullying so that trends in a class or with certain pupils can be monitored and stopped
- inform parents/guardians about bullying incidents and what action is being taken – in serious cases, ask them to come to a meeting to discuss the problem
- call the social services or police, if necessary and appropriate
- make it clear that suspension or exclusion will be considered in serious cases.

What is racist bullying?

Any hostile or offensive action against people because of their skin colour, cultural or religious background or ethnic origin.
  It can include:
- physical, verbal or emotional bullying
- insulting or degrading comments, name calling, gestures, taunts, insults or 'jokes'
- offensive graffiti
- humiliating, excluding, tormenting, ridiculing or threatening
- making fun of the customs, music, accent or dress of anyone from a different culture
- refusal to work with or co-operate with others because they are from a different culture.

Legal position

The Race Relations Act 1976 states that schools and governing bodies have a duty to ensure that students do not face any form of racial discrimination, including attacks and harassment.

• The above information is from Kidscape, see page 41 for address details.

© Kidscape

How young people can help schools tackle bullying

Information from the Anti-Bullying Network

Who is responsible

Teachers and parents have a special responsibility for looking after young people and that includes helping them if they are being bullied at school. But adults cannot do this without help from young people. When someone is bullied at school, other young people who are not directly involved usually know what is going on. Even though they are not involved they could help people who are being bullied. They could encourage them to talk to an adult or could offer to talk to an adult on their behalf. They might be able to

let bullies know that they do not like what they are doing and that they are determined to see it stop. All members of a school community, young and old, have a responsibility to help people who are being bullied and to speak out against bullying behaviour.

Why should young people like you help?

There are many good reasons why young people should help their schools to tackle bullying:
- People who watch bullying but do nothing (they are called bystanders) help the bullies by

providing them with an audience. Who wants to be accused of helping bullies?
- They might want to help a friend, or someone else they know, who is being bullied.
- Some have been bullied themselves in the past and want to stop it happening to other people.
- They may realise that anyone can be bullied – if bullying is not challenged it may be their turn to be victims next.
- Taking part in anti-bullying activities can be enjoyable and worthwhile.

Being cruel isn't cool (a slogan devised in Keith Grammar School).

What if it isn't taken seriously?

If your school is one of those where bullying is still not taken seriously there are things that young people can do to help raise awareness of the problem. Anyone can do this. You just need to be determined to make things change.

Some school students have helped by carrying out questionnaire surveys which can help to show where bullying is happening and how many people are involved. Others have found out about different anti-bullying strategies by reading books and sending away for information. It is best if you can do this as part of the normal activities of the school. Subjects like English, Modern Studies, Religious Studies and PSE (Personal and Social Education) may provide opportunities for work like this. Once your report is ready you could show it to the headteacher, the student council or the school board. This should help everybody to understand that bullying needs to be taken seriously, and that something can be done about it.

How can you help your school?

Many schools are now taking bullying seriously. Here is a list of some of the ways in which teachers and pupils in Scottish schools are dealing with bullying:

- Bully boxes have been set up in some schools. Young people can put notes in these if they are too worried to speak openly about bullying. If your school has boxes like these use them sensibly. Always make sure that anything you write about has really happened.
- Be a buddy to a younger pupil. Older pupils can sometimes volunteer to help new pupils coming into their school by getting to know them and by helping them with any problems
- Special campaigns, such as a 'no-bullying day', can help.
- Some schools have student or pupil councils. You can ask the

council to discuss bullying, even if you are not a member.
- Counselling is a special way of talking to someone. People who are being bullied, or who are bullying others, can be helped by counselling, but only if the counsellor (usually an adult) has had training.
- Some schools have set up peer counselling schemes where young people volunteer to learn how to help other young people.
- Mediation – some schools have introduced schemes where two people who disagree about something agree that a third person, who may be either an adult or another young person, helps to find a solution to a problem. This is helpful in many situations, but not in all cases of

bullying. A bully may refuse to take part because he or she has no interest in ending the bullying. A victim may feel that a negotiated solution is not fair when it is the other person who is entirely in the wrong.
- Taking part in plays and other drama activities can help people to understand what it feels like to be bullied and to think about what they can do to stop it.
- Peer Support is an idea, developed in Australia, in which older students volunteer to discuss things like bullying, friendship or drugs with groups of younger pupils.

Don't leave it to others

If young people leave it all to adults, the problem will never go away. You can help to make your school a better place for everyone, and learn some useful skills at the same time, by joining in with activities like those listed above.

● The above is an extract from the Anti-Bullying Network web site which can be found at www.antibullying.net

© Anti-Bullying Network

Some schools have set up peer counselling schemes where young people volunteer to learn how to help other young people

---

Bullying in the workplace

Information from the Suzy Lamplugh Trust

Bullying used to be considered a problem confined to school students. However, since the incidence of bullying within the workplace was highlighted through the campaign by the indefatigable Andrea Adams before her untimely death in 1995, internal workplace bullying has been seen to be a very real problem. Bullying within the educational sector workplace was particularly highlighted at a meeting in the House of Lords on the subject in March 1996.

Definition

Workplace bullying constitutes unwanted, offensive, humiliating, undermining behaviour towards an individual or groups of employees. Such persistently malicious attacks on personal or professional performance are typically unpredictable, irrational and often unfair. This abuse of power or position can cause such chronic stress and anxiety that people gradually lose belief in themselves, suffering physical ill health and mental distress as a result.

Bullying in the workplace has only recently come to prominence. Workplace bullying affects working conditions, health and safety, domestic life and the right of all to equal opportunity and treatment. Workplace bullying is a separate issue from sexual or racial harassment.

Bullying is a gradual wearing-down process that makes individuals feel demeaned and inadequate, that they can never get anything right and that they are hopeless not only within their work environment but also in their domestic life.

In many instances bullying can be very difficult to detect. It often takes place where there are no witnesses. It can be subtle and devious and often it is difficult for those on the receiving end to confront their perpetrator.

The legal position

The Department of Trade and Industry which is responsible for employment protection legislation states:

'Employers are encouraged to treat their employees with consideration, and bullying and intimidation of employees by their managers is to be deplored. In some circumstances it may indeed be an offence under the Criminal Justice and Public Order Act 1994.

'Employers also have a general duty under health and safety legislation to protect their employees against ill-health caused by work, and this duty extends to stress-related ill-health which might be caused by persistent bullying at work.

'Victims of bullying may also be able to pursue other means of redress through unfair dismissal or discrimination legislation.'

So far the Health and Safety Commission have not accepted that this subject comes under their remit of Violence at Work or under their stress Directorate.

The Trust, however, does feel that it falls within the auspices of Personal Safety and certainly the implementation of a Policy Statement can prove very useful and helpful in establishing principles and practices which help to improve the ethos, efficiency and effectiveness of the service provided to the pupils and public as a whole.

What constitutes bullying within the workplace?

Offensive treatment through vindictive, cruel, malicious or humiliating attempts to undermine an individual.

Persistently negative attacks on personal and professional performance which are typically unpredictable, irrational and often unseen.

This abuse of power or position can cause chronic stress and anxiety to the extent that an employee gradually loses belief in themselves, suffering physical ill-health and mental distress.

Forms of bullying

- Persistent criticism.
- Setting objectives with impossible deadlines.
- Ignoring or excluding an individual by talking only to a third party to isolate another. Freezing people out.
- Withholding information.
- Removing areas of responsibility and giving people menial or trivial tasks to do instead.
- Constantly undervaluing effort.
- Spreading malicious rumours.
- Blocking leave or training applications for no reason.
- Taking credit for other people's ideas.

Identifying a bully

A bully within the work environment is a person who:

- Is likely to have Jekyll and Hyde characteristics.
- Insists their method of working is always right.
- Tells people what requires to be done, then keeps changing the instructions, perhaps in the hope people will make mistakes.
- Shouts at people in order to get things done.
- Persistently picks on, criticises and humiliates people in front of others.
- Gives people tasks that he/she knows they are incapable of achieving.
- Blames everyone but themselves when things go wrong.

Why are people bullied?

A bully will attack certain individuals for a number of reasons, the most prevalent being:

- Popularity amongst colleagues.
- Success.
- Achievement.
- Efficiency.
- Organisational expertise.
- Superior social skills.

Detecting bullying

Supervisory and senior management can detect bullying by recognising certain changes within the working environment, such as:

- High turnover of staff.
- High levels of absenteeism.
- Regular or prolonged sickness absence.

Prevalence of workplace bullying

Approximately one in 10 people (10.5% of employees surveyed) reported themselves as having been bullied at work over the past six months.

Area of work	Bullied now	Bullied last 5 years	Witnessed last 5 years
Brewing industry	1.5%	10.3%	35.3%
Pharmaceuticals	2.5%	17.8%	28.4%
Manufacturing IT	4.2%	22.2%	44.4%
Retailing	6.8%	17.5%	33.1%
Higher education	7.2%	21.1%	41.9%
Hotel industry	7.4%	16.6%	45.4%
Fire service	8.8%	19.8%	42.5%
Manufacturing/engineering	9.8%	22.2%	51.2%
Civil service	9.9%	25.5%	46.1%
Local authority	10.3%	21.4%	41.2%
NHS trusts	10.5%	24.9%	46.2%
Voluntary organisations	11.0%	24.7%	52.8%
Banking	11.5%	24.0%	38.5%
Police service	12.0%	29.0%	45.1%
Dance	14.1%	28.2%	48.2%
Teaching	15.5%	35.4%	54.5%
Post/telecommunications	15.8%	27.1%	47.6%
Prison service	15.9%	31.6%	42.0%
Whole sample	**10.5%**	**24.4%**	**45.2%**

Source: UMIST

- Low morale.
- Loss of initiative.
- Staff looking tense or troubled.

Emotional and physical symptoms linked to bullying

People who are being bullied often suffer from a number of stress-related symptoms such as:

Emotional

- Lost confidence
- Loss of self-esteem
- Lack of motivation
- Irritability/aggression
- Acute anxiety
- Panic attacks
- Anger/murderous feelings
- Depression
- Suicidal thoughts

Physical

- Sleeplessness
- Nausea
- Sweating/shaking
- Palpitations
- Lethargy
- Skin complaints
- Backache
- Stomach/bowel problems
- Migraine/severe headaches

Action to be taken if you are being bullied

You may be able to recognise the early symptoms of bullying and confront the perpetrator by telling them you are not prepared to tolerate their behaviour and you want it to stop.

If you do not or are unable to confront the bully, keep a written record (including dates and details) of all the incidents and attacks on your character, competence and standard of work. Follow this up by sending memos to the perpetrator regarding their behaviour and claims.

Talk about the bullying you are experiencing with your colleagues and if it is happening to them join together, take firm, positive action and make a collective complaint.

If the bullying continues, collate all the evidence you have gathered and present it either to your immediate line supervisor, senior personnel officer, equal opportunities officer or union representative. They will be able to advise you on what to do next.

- The above information is from the Suzy Lamplugh Trust – the leading authority for personal safety. They produce a 'WorldWise' *Book on Safer Travel for Young People* with a 238-country directory, priced at £6.95 + p&p, available from the Trust. You can also visit their web site at www.suzylamplugh.org

© *The Suzy Lamplugh Trust*

Insecurity 'fuels job bullying epidemic'

Survey shows Britain has worst workplace record in Europe

Long hours and growing job insecurity have helped fuel an epidemic of workplace bullying, with one in four employees saying they have been bullied in the past five years, according to the first comprehensive survey of the problem, published yesterday.

Almost half of employees have experienced or seen bullying and one in 10 say they have been bullied in the past six months, the study by Manchester University's Institute of Science and Technology found – response rates significantly higher than elsewhere in Europe.

The survey of 5,300 workers, the largest of its kind ever carried out, and supported by both the TUC and CBI, defined bullying as long-term and persistent negative behaviour, ranging from abuse, humiliation and ridicule to the imposition of unmanageable workloads, unreasonable deadlines and continual fault-finding.

The authors, Cary Cooper and Helge Hoel, found that victims were spread across all levels from senior managers to shopfloor workers, but that 75% of bullies were managers.

Bullying was reported to be most rife in teaching, the prison service, post and telecommunications and the performing arts, and worse in the public than the private sector.

The TUC general secretary, John Monks, called for 'zero tolerance'. John Cridland, human resources director of the CBI, described the extent of workplace bullying as morally unacceptable and bad for business because of its effect on morale, absenteeism, staff turnover and productivity.

The UMIST survey, funded by the British Occupational Health Research Foundation, estimated that victims took an extra seven days off a year compared with other workers.

It also uncovered higher levels

By Seumas Milne,
Labour Editor

of physical and mental ill health among victims and even among those who had only witnessed bullying.

One victim yesterday described how incessant bullying by a manager drove her out of her job in a software firm and landed her in hospital for three weeks with acute stress.

> *One victim yesterday described how incessant bullying by a manager drove her out of her job in a software firm and landed her in hospital for three weeks with acute stress*

'The atmosphere at work was terrible,' she said. 'She would yell and scream at us and undermine everything we did. We weren't able to take responsibility for our own work and we were never given any training. After two years of almost constant bullying, I just felt I couldn't take any more.'

Prof Cooper linked the higher incidence compared with other European countries to the growth of long hours, job insecurity and the effects of 'downsizing' on workloads.

'Bullying then becomes a management style in the face of unmanageable workloads,' he said, adding that overworked and over-stressed managers were now replacing psychopathic bosses as the most common workplace bully.

Typical bullying managers were identified as autocratic and divisive with a tendency to punish on an arbitrary basis.

The authors recommended mechanisms for victims to report bullying without fear of retribution, effective procedures for dealing with complaints, training of managers, and stress audits to avoid work environments which contributed to bullying.

© *Guardian Newspapers Limited 2000*

Witnessing workplace bullying

Nearly half Britain's employees 'have witnessed workplace bullying'

Almost half of Britain's employees (47%) have witnessed bullying at work and one in ten report being bullied in the last six months, a new study has revealed.

The survey, conducted by the University of Manchester Institute of Science and Technology (UMIST) and supported by the TUC and the CBI, suggests the phenomenon contributes to the loss of 18 million working days every year.

5,300 employees from the public, private and voluntary sectors completed the survey, funded by the British Occupational Health Research Foundation, making it the biggest British study of the prevalence and effects of workplace bullying. The key findings show:

- Almost half (47%) the respondents reported witnessing bullying in the last five years. One in ten (10.5%) said they had been bullied in the last six months and one in four (24.4%) said they had been bullied within the last five years.
- An estimated 18 million working days are lost every year because of bullying. Victims of workplace bullying take an average seven extra days off each year than those who are not bullied.
- Bullying affects employees at all levels from workers with no management responsibility (10%) to middle (11%) and senior managers (9%). However, most perpetrators are managers. In three out of four cases (75%) respondents reported being bullied by managers. Just over one-third (37%) reported being bullied by colleagues.
- Over two-thirds of those who were bullied (68%) said they were not the only victims at work.
- Bullying is most common in the prison service (16%), post and telecommunications (16%), teaching (15.5%) and performing arts (14%).
- Bullying is linked to negative management styles. Victims of bullying were more likely to experience autocratic and divisive styles of management than those who hadn't experienced bullying at work.
- Bullying negatively affects morale and productivity. Those who reported being bullied within the last six months consistently report the poorest health, the lowest work motivation and satisfaction, the highest absenteeism figures as well as the lowest productivity, compared to those who were not bullied. Those who witnessed bullying at work were also more likely to report poor health and low morale than those who worked in bullying-free environments.

Professor Cary Cooper and Helge Hoel, the study's authors, want employers to:

- develop procedures for dealing with complaints
- train managers so they are aware of the negative effects of bullying
- undertake regular risk assessments or stress audits to identify bullying at work.

Professor Cary Cooper said: 'The findings in this study show that with better management training and awareness, bullying is avoidable. Workplace bullying not only damages the individual but everybody who experiences it.'

TUC General Secretary John Monks said: 'These shocking new

figures show bullying is rife at work – and that no workplace is immune. The study suggests that bullying is often down to bad management style. That's why it is crucial that unions and employers work together to tackle what is becoming one of Britain's most worrying workplace phenomenona.'

Michael Ladenburg, Chief Executive of the British Occupational Health Research Foundation, said: 'An important part of the study's value lies in the new insights it gives into the many different types of bullying and the cultural changes companies need to bring about if the optimum balance is to be achieved between efficiency and damaging – and potentially costly – pressure in the workplace.'

The findings are based on a national sample of 5,300 respondents from 70 organisations.

Experience of bullying was measured by presenting the respondents with a definition emphasising the negative, long-term and persistent nature of bullying.

The study was advised on by representatives from the public, private and voluntary sectors. Study Advisory Board members include: The Health and Safety Executive, TUC, CBI, The Federation of Small Business, The Institute of Personnel and Development, The Institute of Management, The Employers' Organisation (local government), Co-op, Nat West, Littlewoods, Rover Group, Shell UK, The Suzy Lamplugh Trust, The Andrea Adams Trust, Manufacturing, Science and Finance Union, and the Police Federation.

- A series of TUC rights leaflets, including one on how to tackle bullying at work, are available on the Know Your Rights line 0870 600 4 882. Lines are open every day from 8am-10pm. Calls are charged at the national rate.

© Trades Union Congress (TUC)

Bullying

Information from the Industrial Society

Definition

Workplace bullying is offensive behaviour through vindictive, cruel, malicious or humiliating attempts to undermine the competence, effectiveness, confidence and integrity of an individual or group of employees on a regular and persistent basis.

- Bullying can take many forms and may be re-enforced through authoritarian/hierarchical management systems.
- Bullying cuts across a culture of fairness and opportunity at work. It can occur between colleagues or emanate from a superior.

Background

Traditionally, bullying occurred where management was untrained in the proper skills of motivation and leadership. The dressing down of an employee using derogatory language was accepted practice.

- Today's corporate culture contributes to an increased incidence of workplace bullying.
- The National Workplace Bullying Advice Line reported 3,000 individual cases of bullying at work since 1996.
- A 1997 study of union representatives showed that 66% had either witnessed or experienced bullying at work. In 83% of cases, the bully was the line manager and in 84% of the cases, bullies had bullied before. Few of the companies had anti-bullying policies, even if they were aware of the practice.
- Despite rational belief that bullying is unacceptable behaviour, eradicating the practice, exposing the bully and obtaining redress for victims generally involves a long struggle that can be detrimental to employer and employee.

Key facts

Bullying is recognised as a major cause of stress in the workplace.

- Health and Safety Executive

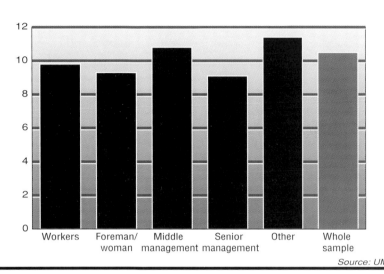

Employees bullied in past six months

Bullying takes place across the organisations irrespective of position.

Source: UMIST

(HSE) figures reveal that, of all stress-related illnesses reported, 10% are caused by poor working relationships where bullying is a frequent complaint.

- The Institute of Management estimates that the cumulative cost – sick pay, lost production and NHS charges – is around £7 billion from an estimated 270,000 absentees caused by work-related stress.
- The HSE corroborate these figures, estimating that 80 million working days are lost at an annual cost of £1 billion – £2 billion to the economy.
- Research by Professor Cary Cooper at UMIST indicates that bullying is a significant factor in all employment-related sickness absence due to stress, accounting for nearly a half of all absences.
- The Trades Union Congress (Health and Safety Division) found, of 8,000 safety representatives, 68% said bullying was the main cause of stress in the workplace, and recommends that prevention should be part of a company's statutory risk assessment procedure.
- Incidence of bullying is greatest

in highly pressurised environments – media, marketing, banking, teaching, the armed forces, the police and emergency services.

State of play

Employers failing to tackle bullying can pay a high price:

- lost time
- lost incentive
- reduced work output and quality of service
- lost resources.
- Employers can face legal costs, punitive damages and loss of reputation. An industrial tribunal in September 1998 ruled against Midland Bank, awarding £4,721 damages and stating that the employer has a duty to implement a policy of fairness at work.
- The Sex Discrimination Act 1975 and Race Relations Act 1976 state that the bully and the organisation may be liable to legal action.
- The Employment Rights Act 1996 can be used if bullying leads to unfair or constructive dismissal.
- Intentional harassment is a criminal offence prohibited by the Public Order Act 1994 and Protection from Harassment Act

1997. To cause a person harassment, alarm or distress by using threatening, abusive, insulting words or disorderly behaviour, or by displaying any writing, sign or other visible representation that is threatening, abusive or insulting is regarded as a breach of law. Should such a case go to Employment Tribunal or to Court, employers and/or the bully may face fines, and possibly a jail sentence.

- All employers have a duty under the Health and Safety at Work Act 1974 to ensure the health, safety and welfare of their staff.
- In *Waltons & Morse v Dorrington* [1997], it was successfully argued that an employer has a duty to create a working environment neither psychologically nor physically damaging to the welfare of employees. Implied here is employment protection from bullying or harassment.

Best practice guidelines

Sound company internal grievance procedures, a health, safety and welfare policy and equal opportunities philosophy helps counter workplace bullying.

- Ensure that all staff are aware that bullying behaviour of any kind will not be tolerated. An understanding should exist of the disciplinary consequences if it arises, and the options by which to raise complaints.
- Identify and publicise possible signs of bullying so that it can be recognised and give examples of unacceptable behaviour in a policy document.
- Senior managers should be encouraged to examine themselves to ensure they are not bullies, particularly as the disease spreads downwards.
- Take all complaints seriously and ensure that the accused is discouraged from retaliation.

- Managers should be issued with strict guidelines on how to discipline a subordinate without bullying.
- Trained staff should handle grievances.
- Bullying is almost always a breach of the employer's duty to ensure health, safety and welfare at work.
- Organisations should monitor turnover, absence and sickness, investigating possible links to bullying.
- Identify areas where bullying may occur, including the content of company e-mail and internal magazines that may be offensive.
- An EU recommendation endorses 'dignity at work' as a code of practice, and the Government's 'Fairness at Work' White Paper seeks to promote employee/employer partnership in order to nurture voluntary understanding and co-operation at work.

© *The Industrial Society*

The low down: workplace bullying

By Bill Saunders

Bullying in the office is something we deplore in the abstract but often condone on a day-to-day basis. Call bullying 'creative tension' and suddenly it becomes acceptable – nobody wants to speak out against creativity.

What makes adult bullying nasty is that it is a 'top-down' process. Inevitable comparisons with the school playground don't really hold water, because the big kid who steals your child's Pokemon cards doesn't pay their salary. Grown-up bullying may be less to do with a rogue individual and more to do with the culture of an entire organisation.

At the British psychological society's occupational psychology conference last week, Iain Coyne of the University of Hull suggested that the correct way to control organisational bullying was to concentrate on the victims.

Coyne and his colleagues have identified a personality profile of the typical employee likely to be bullied. Using personality tests they discovered the potential victim is likely to be 'anxious, unstable, introverted and conscientious'.

This is not to suggest that nature obligingly turns out victims

Grown-up bullying may be less to do with a rogue individual and more to do with the culture of an entire organisation

as fodder for an office-based 'survival of the fittest'. The personality may well be a product of the environment – put bluntly, the victims are likely to be over-careful because they will get shouted at if they get something wrong.

This may be effective in the short term but it is a cruel and depressing way to get things done. The personality profile, Coyne suggests, can be used to identify employees who should be treated in a different way, perhaps through a mentoring scheme or assertiveness training.

Although the emphasis is on the victims, Coyne says it is a 'two-pronged' approach. It also benefits the organisation – managers have a freer hand with their 'creative tension' with less risk of ending up before an industrial tribunal.

© *Guardian Newspapers Limited 2000*

Workplace bullies pile on the agony

Workplace bullies are making life a nightmare for many employees

Jayne Gooch, National Head of Personnel Management Service with Grant Thornton, says that bullying at work is one of the biggest known causes of stress. And, following reports that stress has overtaken the common cold as the biggest cause of sick leave from work, she is urging business owners to ensure that all employees understand the disciplinary consequences if they are found guilty of bullying a fellow member of staff.

'It is easy to underestimate the level of bullying that goes on during working hours,' said Jayne. 'However it is a very real problem which needs addressing.

'When the TUC held a "bad bosses" hotline in December 1997, 38 per cent of callers complained of bullying and all the evidence suggests that the problem has got worse rather than better.'

Although there is currently no specific legislation to protect staff from bullying, Jayne says redress can be found through existing laws.

'There have been calls for the Health and Safety Executive to issue an Approved Code of Practice on stress and to encourage employers to take the subject more seriously. I think we are likely to see legislation that will specifically address the issues of stress and bullying,' she said.

'In the meantime, redress can be found through the Sex, Race and Disability Discrimination Acts. The Employment Rights Act can be used if bullying leads to unfair or constructive dismissal, and the Health and Safety at Work Act 1974 – which demands that employers ensure the health, safety and welfare of their staff – could be deemed to mean protection from bullying.'

Jayne recommends a five-point plan which employers can introduce to combat bullying in the workplace.

Recruitment

Make reasonable checks on an applicant's background and be aware of evidence which may suggest abusive or violent tendencies.

Risk assessment

Analyse the workplace and identify areas where bullying may occur . . . this may include looking out for employees sending intimidating e-mails, disciplinary procedures and grievance procedures.

General employment

Ensure all staff are made aware that bullying of any kind will not be tolerated in the workplace . . . give examples of unacceptable behaviour and ensure all managers are issued with strict guidelines on how to discipline a subordinate without bullying.

Grievance policy

Ensure all staff have a number of options by which to raise complaints, and take all complaints seriously.

Sensitivity

Be aware of the sensitivity of the issue . . . those accused of harassment may be extremely angry about the situation while those who are harassed are likely to feel vulnerable and find it difficult to maintain a sense of self-worth.

'At the end of the day you must ensure that all employees fully understand that disciplinary measures will be taken if anyone is found guilty of bullying a fellow member of staff.

'Your workforce is the most expensive resource you have . . . and when people are not functioning properly, for whatever reason, it can cost you and the business a considerable amount in lost revenue.'

• Grant Thornton is a leading financial and business adviser to owner-managed businesses and their owners. It aims to help them realise their ambitions locally, nationally and internationally – via a network of 42 offices and an international network with representation in over 90 countries.

Please sir, you're a bully

More than half of our teachers want to leave the job – that's hardly surprising when one in six has been bullied

By Jim Pollard

In the average school, nearly one in six has been bullied in the past six months. No surprise there, perhaps – kids have been bullying each other since Cain and Abel – except this figure is not for pupils, it is for teachers.

Bullying is a growing problem in the workplace, particularly among professionals who are supposed to be caring for others such as teachers, prison officers, doctors and nurses. A recent survey at the Manchester School of Management (UMIST) found that one in four of us had been bullied at work in the past five years. In teaching it is one in three.

The scale of the problem is often underestimated because, understandably, victims are reluctant to talk about bullying. Cary Cooper, the professor of organisational psychology who carried out the research, calculates that it is responsible for 18 million lost working days every year and causes 30-50 per cent of work-related stress illness. Ultimately, employers pay as well as employees. In a landmark High Court ruling in 1994 a social worker was awarded £175,000 following a stress-related breakdown and now an informal survey of personal injury and employment lawyers suggests more than a third of all work-related stress cases are about bullying.

'In my view there are two types of bully,' says Cooper. 'The psychopathic bully has low self-esteem and may not be particularly good at their job. He or she bullies to enhance their status. It's a personality dysfunction and the numbers are relatively small and stable. The other type is the overloaded bully who has too much to do themselves and dumps on others. This sort of bullying is increasing.'

He draws a distinction between European and Anglo-American corporate cultures. 'Downsizing, short-term contracts and long working hours all help short-term global competitiveness, but coupled with increasing technology overload from e-mails, faxes and mobile phones, they create a climate in which employees are overloaded and bullying is inevitable,' he says. 'This is unhealthy for UK plc in the long term.'

> **Bullying is a growing problem in the workplace, particularly among professionals who are supposed to be caring for others such as teachers**

It has certainly been unhealthy for teachers. The profession offers a lesson in the long-term impact of bullying. As assistant secretary of the NAS/UWT teaching union, Les Roberts conducted a major survey of staffroom bullying in 1997. He

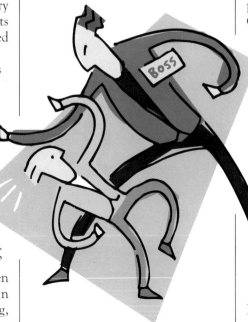

believes the problem is getting worse and the figures bear him out. A recent *Guardian*/ICM poll found that more than half of teachers intend to leave the profession within the next 10 years including a third of those under 35. Cary Cooper is not surprised. 'In our survey, those who are bullied consistently report the poorest health, the lowest work motivation, satisfaction and productivity and the highest absenteeism and intentions to leave.'

Better employers are recognising this. 'We've had a bullying policy since 1994,' says Barry Gibson, chief executive of the retailer Littlewoods. 'Only in a workplace free from bullying can our potential as individuals and as a company be fully realised. I believe it was reflected in our success at the 1999 Institute of Personnel and Development People Management Awards.' The company was overall winner.

Cooper is particularly concerned about public-sector bullying. A survey by the union Unison found that two-thirds had experienced or witnessed bullying. 'Many people in the private sector may feel they're paid enough to be able to put up with some bullying,' says Cooper, 'but that's not the case in the public sector, where management training is also less good. I've never been trained for my higher education management responsibilities, and how many school headteachers have? The odd day isn't enough.' He calls for better management training, stress audits, a safe whistle-blowing mechanism and an effective complaints procedure.

So where does the bullying buck stop? 'The more hierarchical a profession, the easier it is for bullying to cascade down,' says Cooper. The NAS/UWT's Roberts agrees. 'There's increasing pressure on schools from outside,' he says, 'particularly on headteachers and they pass this pressure down the line.'

Cooper identifies certain management styles as 'bullying'. These include naming and shaming, whereby poor performance is drawn to wider attention. 'Public ostracism creates a bad atmosphere among employees. Weaker ones become fearful and defensive, better ones leave,' he says.

So how can you tell if your bullying boss is psychopathic or overloaded? Cooper believes it depends on whether they have always bullied. 'If your boss bullies regardless of circumstances, it may be psychopathic,' he says. 'If it varies with workload, he or she is probably overloaded.' Will this cheer up the 200,000 teachers who are looking to leave the job?

On the receiving end

'She abused me so much I burst into tears.' Tony teaches at an inner London secondary school. His name has been changed because his borough disciplines employees who talk to the media.

'I've been bullied in many ways – some are subtle, some aren't. There's humiliation. On one occasion I was belittled by the headteacher in front of a pupil in her office. She later denied knowing he had been there.

'There's death by memo – any slight slip and instantly there's a memo reprimanding you. There's death by monitoring – our lessons and our students' books are inspected constantly. Excessively. The kids are even asked to grade our performance, which undermines authority. The worst occasion was when I'd just returned after being off with stress and the head abused me so much I burst into tears. She physically prevented me from leaving her office by blocking the door. I could only have got out by assaulting her. Now I never see her without someone accompanying me.

'I don't have a problem with female managers. My head of department is a woman and it's great. It's this head. She's overworked, makes mistakes in the heat of the moment and can't admit she's wrong.

'I've had time off for stress and spent the last half-term not sleeping. It's affected my relationship with my wife and my kids. Without the support of my union I couldn't have carried on.

'Don't get me wrong. I love teaching – in the classroom, with a good class I have a lovely time – and I don't believe I'm a bad teacher.'

Bullying barometer
You are being bullied when:
- your presence or opinions are ignored
- you are denied information about your performance
- you are humiliated or ridiculed
- you are given an unmanageable workload
- you are given unreasonable deadlines
- your work is excessively monitored
- gossip and rumour are spread about you
- faults are continually found with your work.

• The TUC Know Your Rights line (0870 600 4882) can advise on bullying (charged at national rate).

• First published in *The Observer*, April 2000.

How to . . . recognise a bully

By Neasa MacErlean

1. **Accept** that most people (including you) have the potential to be bullies. Most bullies are appalled if they find out how other people regard them. You are more likely to humiliate and undermine others if you are unhappy or resentful; if you have been treated badly; if you work in a climate of fear; if you are in a position to abuse others; and if you let your emotions take over at times.

Physical abuse and bullying have occurred in many children's homes where an imbalance of power left the children unprotected.

2. **Look** for the conditions in which bullying flourishes: intense competition between colleagues to reach sales targets or avoid redundancy; or hierarchical structures where subordinates have little power to answer back. Many occupations have institutionalised bullying – by giving power to the hectoring army sergeant, for example, or the battleaxe headmistress. 'Some bullies just like to have power over others,' says psychologist Sandi Mann, author of *Psychology Goes to Work*. 'For some it's just a way of managing: they don't know any other way.'

3. **Ask** yourself how often you are criticised by juniors and peers. If people are scared to say anything critical to you, the chances are you frighten them, which means you have bullying tendencies.

4. **Examine** your emotional response to work. If you get depressed by it, sleep badly, hate Sunday evenings, something is clearly wrong and you may be the subject of bullying. Many victims do not recognise the fact – perhaps because they are used to being bullied at home or at school, or they think it would seem wimpish to complain. Men are particularly scared of admitting to being bullied: harassment is a more comfortable word.

5. **Check** to see that you are not abusing your power. A sure sign of your emotional corruption is if you treat subordinates in a way that you would never treat your superiors. The healthiest people will question their own bosses but treat their staff with respect and encouragement. If you have to shout at someone, it should be your boss, never your staff.

Occupational bullying

Information from Carole Spiers MIHE MISMA, Occupational Stress Counsellor, Carole Spiers Associates

Definition of bullying

The *Oxford Dictionary* definition of a 'bully' is: 'A person who hurts, persecutes or intimidates weaker people.'

The bully is described as 'a person using strength or power to coerce others by fear'. While neither is a particularly laudable character trait, a bossy person will usually acknowledge that this is the way they are if it is drawn to their attention. Being bossy is certainly aggressive, but this type of behaviour is generally short-lived and most people can learn to cope with it without too much difficulty in a working environment. 'Bossiness', however, turns to bullying when professional abrasiveness becomes tainted with an element of personal vindictiveness.

In a place of work, being a bully is about persistently snapping and finding fault. A bully is unlikely to listen to people's opinions and ideas, considers nothing and talks over others when they are trying to raise a point. In many cases, the bullying boss will not possess the social skills, which equip a person with the art of compromise. A person in an ultimate position of power is unlikely to be successfully challenged. There is also an assumption in many organisations that the more senior you are, the less management training you need.

Differentiating between bossiness and bullying within the workforce is not as difficult as it may appear. Bossiness is unlikely to affect people's mental and physical health. In general, everyone is on the receiving end, and if the person becomes too overbearing, they can be challenged without fear of reprisal. Even a good moan among colleagues will relieve the tension, and at least everyone can confront it together.

Being bullied is an isolating experience. It tends not to be openly discussed in case this poses the risk of further ill treatment. Those who are the prime targets often feel ashamed to discuss it with colleagues because their professional credibility is being called into question. The difficulty for the individual arises because bullying is swept under the all-embracing title of intimidation. What may be identified as the mildest form of intimidation is none the less very disturbing when you are the victim. As bullying moves up the Richter scale of aggression, and gets a severe grip on any group or individual, its physical effects are simply more severe.

The costs of bullying in the workplace

- high staff turnover
- absenteeism
- regular or prolonged sickness absence
- staff looking tense or troubled
- a change in atmosphere
- reduced productivity
- less concern with quality
- low morale
- loss of initiative
- lack of creative input

Examples of bullying behaviour

- Verbally abusive behaviour in public and private
- Persistent criticism in open forum
- Intimidation
- Deriding comments
- Ridiculing
- Ignoring
- Unfair treatment
- Undervaluing personal effort

- Browbeating
- Encouraged to feel guilty
- Making someone feel inadequate
- Excluding to the point of non-communication
- Subject to excessive monitoring, supervision, recording, snooping etc.
- Denied annual leave, sickness leave
- Have their responsibility increased but their authority removed
- Increased volume of workload
- Lack of support and backup
- Have their work plagiarised
- Insistence that the bully's way of working is always right
- Tell people what needs to be done, then keep changing the instructions, perhaps in the hope that they will make mistakes
- Give people tasks that they know are incapable of achieving
- Shout at staff to get things done

The emotional effects of bullying behaviour

Employees can be subject to fear, stress and anxiety, which may put great strains on personal and family life. It can lead to illness, increased absenteeism, an apparent lack of commitment, poor performance and even resignation. All these have a direct impact on organisation effectiveness.

No employer should underestimate the damage, tension and conflict within the workplace which harassment creates. The result is not just poor morale but higher labour turnover, reduced productivity, lower efficiency and divided teams. Although the effects may be difficult to quantify, they will eventually show through in the performance of the organisation.

A distinguishing characteristic of bullying behaviour is that employees subjected to it are very vulnerable and are often reluctant to complain. They may be too embarrassed or unsure as to how to make a complaint, or concerned that it will be trivialised. They may fear reprisals. The victims of bullying behaviour may not want attention focused on the situation: they just want the unwanted behaviour to stop, so they suffer in silence.

Work is often disrupted since the victim is unable to concentrate on their tasks. Erratic timekeeping and absenteeism are commonplace. Tasks involving co-operation between people will suffer and group cohesiveness will be lost.

How does the person feel?

People who are being bullied can feel helpless. They believe that nothing can be done to alleviate the situation and consequently take no action. Most people believe that they would end up being labelled as trouble-makers. The person can feel foolish that they can't cope with the situation.

Sufferers will also feel guilty for a number of reasons. They may feel that they have contributed to the situation in some way and constantly review their behaviour and the content of conversation in an effort to pinpoint what initiated the attention. The reality is that they are unlikely to have caused the situation.

Feelings associated with being bullied

Physical
- Feeling sick
- Sweating, shaking
- Disturbed sleep
- Palpitations
- Loss of energy
- Stomach/bowel problems
- Severe headaches
- Loss of libido
- Minor aches and pains

Emotional
- Anxiety
- Irritability
- Panic attacks
- Depression
- Anger, murderous feelings
- Lack of motivation
- Loss of confidence
- Feeling of isolation
- Reduced self-esteem

> *The victims of bullying behaviour may not want attention focused on the situation: they just want the unwanted behaviour to stop, so they suffer in silence*

Tactics for the person feeling bullied

- Stand firm if you come under verbal attack. Tell the bully that you will not tolerate personal remarks.
- Remember that this type of person is likely to be at their worst when they feel under pressure.
- Remain confident in your own judgement and ability.
- If you clash over work contributions, keep calm and say

what has to be said quietly and coherently.
- If objectives or instructions are unclear, ask for written clarification. Explain that this will provide an *aide-mémoire* to help you achieve the aims within the given time.

Verdicts of recent bullying cases

1999 – Suicide due to bullying behaviour
A verdict of suicide was made by a Surrey coroner after stating that an employee's job at Shroder's Bank had subjected him to pressure or bullying. 'It would seem that Mr Mason was subject to some sort of bullying and pressure that made life very difficult for him.

1999 – Noonan vs. Liverpool City Council
£84,000 paid in damages to a Home Help Supervisor who quit her job claiming she was suffering from stress after being bullied for five years by a colleague.

Bullying survey – response

Levels of bullying were found to vary greatly between occupations and industries.

Area of work	Total sample	Returned questionnaires	Response rate, %
Public sector			
NHS trusts	1,069	535	50.5%
Post/telecomms	1,000	273	27.3
Civil service	250	141	56.4%
Higher education	1,072	487	45.4%
Teaching	1,000	426	42.6%
Local authority	924	388	42.0%
Police service	1,000	483	48.3%
Fire service	1,167	520	44.6%
Prison service	1,000	471	47.1%
Total public sector	**8,482**	**3,724**	**43.9%**
Manufacturing			
Manufacturing/engineering	177	82	46.3%
Manufacturing. IT	475	189	39.8%
Brewing	160	68	42.5%
Pharmaceuticals	350	197	56.3%
Total manufacturing	**1,162**	**536**	**45.1%**
Services			
Hotels	493	163	32.7%
Retailing	855	354	41.4%
Banking	820	262	32.0%
Voluntary organisations	317	123	38.8%
Dance	196	85	43.4%
Total services	**2,681**	**987**	**36.8%**
Total sample	**12,350**	**5,288**	**42.8%**

Source: UMIST

2000 – Mcleod vs. Test Valley Borough Council

£203,000 awarded for work-related stress due to bullying in the workplace.

FACT:

2000 UMIST survey supported by TUC and CBI: Bullying is contributing to the loss of 18 million working days every year.

In conclusion

The following suggestions give a pro-active approach in dealing with bullying in the workplace:

- watch the workplace for a change

The 2000 UMIST survey supported by TUC and CBI: Bullying is contribu-ting to the loss of 18 million working days every year

---

in atmosphere among staff when cheerfulness turns to virtual silence ('walking the floor' style

of management will be counter-productive if the boss is a bully).

- use stress/culture audits or upward assessments to identify problem areas.
- introduce agenda-free meetings to provide a platform for troubled staff.
- in exit interviews, include the specific question: 'have you experienced bullying in this organisation?'
- For more information please see www.csa-stress.co.uk or contact www.info@csa-stress.co.uk

The likely victims

'Submissive worriers' the likely victims of bullying at work

Conscientious workers who worry about their professional ability and are shy and submissive among colleagues are the most likely to suffer workplace bullying, research revealed yesterday.

Psychologists have pinpointed the personality trait they believe make people susceptible to an increasingly prevalent form of bullying. Figures from the TUC suggest 5m people will be bullied at some point in their careers.

The research, conducted by psychologists at the University of Hull and released at the conference in Brighton, was based on personality tests of 120 workers in two organisations, one public and one private, in Dublin.

Half those tested had been bullied for at least six months and half had never experienced victimisation.

The test measured how in-dependent, conscientious, extrovert and stable the workers were.

'Victims were very much more submissive, low in independence, very introverted and somewhat highly conscientious,' said Eain Coyne, a lecturer in psychology and the report's co-author.

'But the biggest difference we found between them and those who

---

By Sarah Hall

---

haven't been bullied was that they were extremely anxious and neurotic.'

Mr Coyne continued: 'We are not saying personality causes bullying because that could be due to the competitive nature of the organisation. Personality gives indications as to who is bullied and not why bullying occurs.

Most frequent, regular negative acts

Daily, weekly and monthly

Negative acts	Currently bullied (%)	Not currently bullied (%)
1. Opinions ignored	53.6	9.9
2. Withholding information	49.9	17.2
3. Unmanageable workload	45.9	18.4
4. Unreasonable deadlines	38.4	14.4
5. Ordered to work below competence	36.4	11.8
6. Fault finding	34.9	2.4
7. Humiliated or ridiculed	33.8	3.2
8. Facing hostility	32.6	3.4
9. Excessive monitoring	31.5	7.0
10. Spreading gossip	31.1	4.6
11. Insults or offensive remarks	30.6	4.3
12. Removal of responsibility	29.2	7.3

Source: UMIST

'But the combination of personality traits emerging from this study may be a trigger to the bully to choose this individual to bully rather than someone else.'

The psychologists now hope to build on research into the characteristics of bullies.

'It could be there is a tension between the characters of bullies and the characters of victims which leads to this bullying,' said Mr Coyne.

The academics also hope to adapt the commercial test so that employers can determine if potential employees are likely to be bullied, and then introduce preventative measures.

'Organisations could offer mentoring techniques and assertiveness training for those most at risk,' he said.

Passive bullying

Why office bullying can be just as traumatic for the witness as for the victim

Workers given a tongue-lashing by the boss are not the only ones who suffer stress, claim psychologists.

Angry scenes in the workplace can have 'profoundly disturbing implications' for colleagues who witness them.

As a result, employers could be facing compensation claims over a new phenomenon – passive bullying.

Flare-ups at work tended to have a 'spreading effect' so that everyone became involved, said occupational psychologist Professor Cary Cooper.

'This is passive bullying,' he told an audience of union officials at TUC headquarters in London yesterday.

A study by Professor Cooper and fellow academics at the University of Manchester School of Management found that one in four workers had been subjected to verbal abuse by bosses at some stage over the last five years.

One in ten of those questioned claimed to have been bullied in the last six months.

However, nearly 47 per cent reported that over the same period they had been involved in passive bullying by witnessing angry scenes in the office or on the shopfloor.

If the figures were applied to the entire UK workforce, it would mean there have been more than ten million passive bullying 'victims' since 1995.

Employers fear the next step could be unions encouraging workers to lodge claims, bringing a fresh surge of tribunal cases in the already booming compensation culture.

The study, which questioned 5,300 employees in 70 organisations,

By David Norris, Industrial Correspondent

claimed that the level of 'conventional' workplace bullying was now huge.

Statistics indicated that around six million people had been subjected to direct verbal abuse in the workplace over the last five years.

One in ten of those questioned claimed to have been bullied in the last six months

The resulting stress and low morale, the academics suggested, could be manifesting itself in as many as 18 million working days a year being lost through absenteeism.

Cash awards to bullied workers are becoming commonplace. In July, Cath Noonan, a £19,000-a-year home help employed by Liverpool City Council, received £84,000 in an out-of-court settlement after being bullied by a colleague for five years.

In 1998, deputy head teacher Anthony Ratcliffe won £100,000 after claiming he was bullied by colleagues at a primary school in Tenby, South Wales.

John Monks, leader of the TUC, which backed the university study, said: 'Annual reports by companies like to stress that their staff are their greatest asset.

'This research shows that some workplace practices seem to have come straight from the pages of Dickens.'

The study was supported by the Confederation of British Industry, which said that making an employee's life a misery 'is not only morally unacceptable but is also bad for business'.

OUR STAFF – –ARE OUR GREATEST ASSET... –IS THAT THE BULLIES OR THE BULLIED?

Spotting the signs

Information from the Graphical Paper Media Union (GPMU)

Workplace bullies can pick on anyone: man or woman, black or white. It is that arbitrary. Bullies often get away with it by making victims think it's their fault. Learn to spot the signs and fight back.

What is bullying?

Workplace bullying is generally vindictive, cruel, malicious or humiliating behaviour towards an individual or even a group of employees. It is demeaning and can cause untold stress and suffering to those on the receiving end.

There's nothing new in this – what is new is acknowledging that it reaches far beyond the playground, and crops up where you may least expect it. It may occur between workers but equally it can be the abuse of authority by management. It may reflect a management style that is autocratic and based on telling people what to do rather than allowing them any personal initiative.

Bullies can be motivated by a number of things such as lack of self-confidence, envy towards other people's abilities, success and popularity or they may take a completely irrational dislike to an aspect of someone's personality or their way of doing things.

Workplace danger signs

Evidence shows that bullying is most likely to occur in workplaces where there is/are:

- an extremely competitive environment
- fear of redundancy
- fear for one's position
- a culture of promoting oneself by putting colleagues down
- envy among colleagues
- an authoritarian style of management and supervision
- organisational change and uncertainty
- little participation
- lack of training
- de-skilling

- no respect for others and their point of view
- poor work relationships generally
- no clear codes for acceptable conduct
- excessive workloads and demands on people
- impossible targets or deadlines
- no procedures for resolving problems.

Bullying can take many forms such as: open aggression, threats, shouting, abuse, ridicule, excessive supervision, and constant criticism.

How bullies operate

Bullies may also take the credit for a person's work, never the blame, over-rule a person's authority, remove whole areas of work responsibility from the person, give them only routine tasks which are well below their capabilities, set impossible targets, constantly change a person's duties without telling them and then criticise or discipline the person for not meeting those demands, withhold information, ostracise and marginalise their target, exclude the person from discussions or decisions, spread malicious rumours, refuse requests for training or block a person's promotion.

Bullying may occur in front of other employees who then become too afraid of becoming the next target to do anything to help the person being bullied, but sometimes it can be more subtle and harder to detect. It can often happen where there are no witnesses. The victim is often too afraid to complain and worried that they will not be believed in any case.
© *Graphical, Paper & Media Union (GPMU)*

Bullying in workplace is costing UK £2bn per year

By Amanda Kelly

Businesses were urged yesterday to stamp out bullying in the workplace after a report said the problem was costing British industry £2bn a year.

Up to 19 million working days are lost because workers are suffering from verbal and physical threats, offensive remarks and humiliation, said the guide published by the London Chamber of Commerce.

Overworked managers are highlighted as the group most likely to be guilty of bullying and, accordingly, many employees are too afraid to make formal complaints and choose to stay at home instead.

Those who do reach the workplace are more likely to make mistakes or have an accident. Even the work of employees who are not the victims of bullying, but who witness their colleagues being mistreated, is likely to suffer. High staff turnover, absenteeism, repeated minor illnesses and poor work performance are all signs of companies where bullies are employed.

Simon Sperryn, chief executive of the London Chamber of Commerce, said: 'Bullying is often a hidden problem but it needs to be rooted out.'

Examples of bullying set out in the guide include unjustified criticism, setting unattainable targets, undervaluing someone's work and monitoring work unnecessarily.

© *The Independent Newspaper Ltd, 2000*

Half the population are bullied

. . . most people only realise it when they read this

Read through the following check-lists and learn how to recognise the bullies in your life and the harm they cause to you and others.

Where are people bullied?

- at work by their manager or co-workers or subordinates, or by their clients (bullying, workplace bullying, mobbing, work abuse, harassment, discrimination)
- at home by their partner or parents or siblings or children (bullying, assault, domestic violence, abuse, verbal abuse)
- at school (bullying, harassment, assault)
- in the care of others, such as in hospital, convalescent homes, care homes, residential homes (bullying, harassment, assault)
- in the armed forces (bullying, harassment, discrimination, assault)
- by those in authority (harassment, abuse of power)
- by neighbours and landlords (bullying, harassment)
- by strangers (harassment, stalking, assault, sexual assault, rape, grievous bodily harm, murder)

How do you know if you're being bullied?

Bullying differs from harassment and assault in that the latter can result from a single incident or small number of incidents – which everybody recognises as harassment or assault – whereas bullying tends to be an accumulation of many small incidents over a long period of time. Each incident tends to be trivial, and on its own and out of context does not constitute an offence or grounds for disciplinary or grievance action. So . . .

What is bullying?

- constant nit-picking, fault-finding and criticism of a trivial nature – the triviality, regularity and frequency betray bullying; often there is a grain of truth (but only a grain) in the criticism to fool you into believing the criticism has validity, which it does not; often, the criticism is based on distortion, mis-representation or fabrication
- simultaneous with the criticism, a constant refusal to acknowledge you and your contributions and achievements or to recognise your existence and value
- constant attempts to undermine you and your position, status, worth, value and potential
- where you are in a group (e.g. at work), being singled out and treated differently; for instance, everyone else can get away with murder but the moment you put a foot wrong – however trivial – action is taken against you
- being isolated and separated from colleagues, excluded from what's going on, marginalised, overruled, ignored, sidelined, frozen out, sent to Coventry
- being belittled, demeaned and patronised, especially in front of others
- being humiliated, shouted at and threatened, often in front of others
- being overloaded with work, or having all your work taken away and replaced with either menial tasks (filing, photocopying, minute taking) or with no work at all
- finding that your work – and the credit for it – is stolen and plagiarised
- having your responsibility increased but your authority taken away
- having annual leave, sickness leave, and – especially – compassionate leave refused
- being denied training necessary for you to fulfil your duties
- having unrealistic goals set, which change as you approach them
- ditto deadlines which are changed at short notice – or no notice – and without you being informed until it's too late
- finding that everything you say and do is twisted, distorted and misrepresented
- being subjected to disciplinary procedures with verbal or written warnings imposed for trivial or fabricated reasons and without proper investigation
- being coerced into leaving through no fault of your own, constructive dismissal, early or ill-health retirement, etc.

How do I recognise a bully?

Most bullying is traceable to one person, male or female – bullying is not a gender issue. Bullies are often clever people (especially female bullies) but you can be clever too.

Who does this describe in your life?

- Jekyll and Hyde nature – vicious and vindictive in private, but innocent and charming in front of witnesses; no one can (or wants to) believe this individual has a vindictive nature – only the current target sees both sides
- is a convincing, compulsive liar and when called to account, will make up anything spontaneously to fit their needs at that moment
- uses lots of charm and is always plausible and convincing when peers, superiors or others are present; the motive of the charm is deception and its purpose is to compensate for lack of empathy
- relies on mimicry to convince others that they are a 'normal' human being but their words, writing and deeds are hollow, superficial and glib
- displays a great deal of certitude and self-assuredness to mask their insecurity
- excels at deception
- exhibits unusual, inappropriate attitudes to sexual matters or sexual behaviour; underneath the charming exterior there are often suspicions or intimations of sexual harassment, sex discrimination or sexual abuse (sometimes racial prejudice as well)
- exhibits much controlling behaviour and is a control freak
- displays a compulsive need to criticise whilst simultaneously refusing to acknowledge, value and praise others
- when called upon to share or address the needs and concerns of others, responds with impatience, irritability and aggression
- often has an overwhelming, unhealthy and narcissistic need to portray themselves as a wonderful, kind, caring and compassionate person, in contrast to their behaviour and treatment of others; the bully is oblivious to the discrepancy between how they like to be seen (and believe they are seen), and how they are actually seen
- has an overbearing belief in their qualities of leadership but cannot distinguish between leadership (maturity, decisiveness, assertive-

---

Most bullying is traceable to one person, male or female – bullying is not a gender issue. Bullies are often clever people (especially female bullies) but you can be clever too

---

ness, trust and integrity) and bullying (immaturity, impulsiveness, aggression, distrust and deceitfulness)

- when called to account, immediately and aggressively denies everything, then counterattacks with distorted or fabricated criticisms and allegations; if this is insufficient, quickly feigns victimhood, often by bursting into tears (the purpose is to avoid answering the question and thus evade accountability by manipulating others through the use of guilt)
- is also . . . aggressive, devious, manipulative, spiteful, vengeful, doesn't listen, can't sustain mature adult conversation, lacks a conscience, shows no remorse,

---

Getting to grips with bullying

Do you dread going to work for fear of being humiliated or bullied in front of your workmates? If so, you're not alone. As many as five million people have been bullied at work, according to a recent TUC poll.

The NOP survey asked if people had been bullied themselves or if they were aware of bullying where they work, or used to work. More than one in ten respondents (11 per cent) were now or had been victims of workplace bullying and over a quarter (27 per cent) were aware bullying went on where they worked or used to work.

Men and women are equally likely to be victims of bullying, and it's a problem at every level of work, with pretty much the same amount of harassment going on among unskilled workers (9 per cent) as among skilled blue-collar (11 per cent) and skilled white-collar (10 per cent) workers.

GPMU is working hard to challenge workplace bullying. The union has negotiated a Dignity at Work clause in companies which are part of the British Printing Industries Federation, which states that staff must not be subjected to racial or sexual harassment or bullying.

'The dignity at work clause has proved effective for our members,' says GPMU equality policy adviser Tricia Dawson.

Where the anti-bullying guidelines are negotiated into agreements, they must cover all employees and spell out that bullying is a disciplinary offence. 'One member of the BPIF found to their cost that it is not good enough simply to have the guidelines in the national agreement – industrial tribunals expect those guidelines to be adhered to,' Tricia says.

In addition, the union appoints lay women members within branches to act as points of contact for those suffering from harassment at work. The liaison officers can help branch officers resolve bullying problems and refer members to counselling services when necessary.

'We felt it was important that the liaison officers were women, in order to encourage women members suffering harassment and bullying to come forward without the additional ordeal of having to confide in a male official,' Tricia explains.

© Graphical, Paper & Media Union (GPMU)

is drawn to power, emotionally cold and flat, humourless, joyless, ungrateful, dysfunctional, disruptive, divisive, rigid and inflexible, selfish, insincere, insecure, immature and deeply inadequate, especially in interpersonal skills.

I estimate one person in thirty has this behaviour profile. I describe them as a socialised psychopath, or sociopath: a violent, aggressive but intelligent individual who expresses their violence psychologically (constant criticism etc.) rather than physically (assault).

What does bullying do to my health?

Bullying causes injury to health and makes you ill. How many of these symptoms do you have?

- constant high levels of stress and anxiety
- frequent illness such as viral infections especially flu and glandular fever, colds, coughs, chest, ear, nose and throat infections (stress plays havoc with your immune system)
- aches and pains in the joints and muscles with no obvious cause; also back pain with no obvious cause and which won't go away or respond to treatment
- headaches and migraines
- tiredness, exhaustion, constant fatigue
- sleeplessness, nightmares, waking early, waking up more tired than when you went to bed
- flashbacks and replays, obsessiveness, can't get the bullying out of your mind
- irritable bowel syndrome
- skin problems such as eczema, psoriasis, athlete's foot, ulcers, shingles, urticaria
- poor concentration, can't concentrate on anything for long
- bad or intermittently-functioning memory, forgetfulness, especially with trivial day-to-day things
- sweating, trembling, shaking, palpitations, panic attacks
- tearfulness, bursting into tears regularly and over trivial things
- uncharacteristic irritability and angry outbursts
- hypervigilance (feels like but is not paranoia), being constantly on edge
- hypersensitivity, fragility, isolation, withdrawal
- reactive depression, a feeling of woebegoneness, lethargy, hopelessness, anger, futility and more
- shattered self-confidence, low self-worth, low self-esteem, loss of self-love, etc.

• The above is an extract from the web site www.successunlimited.co.uk
© Tim Field

Why bullying at work has to stop

You don't expect intimidation and cruelty in a civilised workplace, but adult bullying ruins the lives of up to one in four working women

Getting dressed, organised and out of the house in the morning can be stressful enough for most of us. But for many women what lies ahead is much worse. Too nervous even to eat breakfast, they arrive at work feeling sick, head pounding, hands wet and mouth dry with fear.

Many of these women may have worked happily for the same company for years – only now they've become part of a growing trend, falling foul of a workplace bully who makes their lives unbearable.

Incredibly, according to a *Good Housekeeping* survey published in March, one in four women has suffered at the hands of a bully during her working life. And many others have seen it happen to friends and colleagues and witnessed how it can lead to severe loss of confidence, depression or, in extreme cases, a breakdown.

Research by the University of Manchester School of Management provides an even more disturbing picture. Almost half of the people they questioned said they'd witnessed bullying in the workplace in the past year, with one in 10 admitting it had happened to them within the past six months.

Worse still, these figures are on the increase. Last year the MSF (the Manufacturing, Science and Finance union) described bullying as 'spreading through the workplace like a cancer'.

Does this sound like your boss?

While being bullied is likely to make you feel insecure and lacking in confidence, these are, perversely, the very reasons behind it. According to clinical psychologist Professor Robert Edelmann, 'Bullies tend to feel threatened. They may be afraid of losing their job or lack confidence in doing the job assigned to them, so exert more authority to try to make people think they're better at it than they actually are.'

Bullying behaviour can be rooted in childhood experiences of being bullied, or of always getting your own way. 'Whatever the root cause, bullies are likely to be envious of another's ability, success or popularity,' says Professor Edelmann. 'And the only way they can see to sabotage that is to undermine the other person.'

The actions of a bully can have devastating consequences. They take over their victim's life, not just at work but at home too, as bullying can lead to a string of debilitating symptoms including disturbed sleep, nausea, headaches, palpitations, panic attacks, stomach problems and frequent infections.

All this is estimated to cost the taxpayer between £5 and £12 billion per year – around £500 for every working adult. According to the

Andrea Adams Trust, a charity that aims to reduce the incidences of workplace bullying by raising awareness, one of the hardest things is to admit you're being bullied. 'If you've always believed yourself to be confident, strong and good at your job, it's hard to admit you can't cope with someone else's behaviour or continual criticism,' explains spokesperson Val Wallace. 'People often wonder if they're being too sensitive.'

Can the law protect you from a bully?

Incredibly, bullying in the workplace is still not recognised as a problem by British law. If you complained about a bully's actions, got nowhere and were forced to leave your job as a result, chances are they'd still be no satisfaction for you if you went down the legal route.

Tim Field, author of *Bully in Sight* (Success Unlimited, £12.95) and founder of the National Work-

place Bullying Advice Line, says: 'Bullying has fallen through a huge legal loophole. Unless you can prove it's directly related to your sex, race or a disability, there is no law to cover it.

'If you were sacked maybe because the increasing pressure you were under resulted in poor performance or excessive absenteeism, you could try to claim for unfair dismissal,' says Field. 'Or, if you handed in your notice because it all got to be too much, you could claim for constructive dismissal. But it hardly seems worth it when you consider that it will take at least two years, during which time getting another job will be hard because you'll be seen as a trouble-maker. And compensation payouts are paltry – £2500, on average.'

A victim's only other option is to fight under the Duty of Care law, which can result in higher payouts, but this is a lengthy, expensive process that often takes as long as five years. You'll need a solicitor, and you'll have to gather sufficient evidence to prove that the bullying has caused you physical and mental stress, which can be very difficult. All in all, the whole process could cost you thousands. What's needed is a much more accessible system of redress for victims of bullying in the workplace; something, for example, like the one open to those who have suffered from racial or sexual discrimination.

The only other situation in which you're currently likely to get a substantial payment – or one that

---

Julie's story

Julie*, 47, has worked as a secretary in an NHS Trust for 21 years. She had always enjoyed her job until the arrival of a new boss in the department.

'In my experience, bullies are clever people. They play colleagues off against each other until the atmosphere is so tense that going to work feels like a perpetual visit to the dentist. My bully – my manager's boss – completely obliterated the office where I worked. Sometimes she criticised me to my face, other times indirectly, telling my manager to tell me that my skirt was too short, make-up too heavy and perfume too strong. Towards the end she even made me tell my boss when I needed to go to the toilet. I was so stressed that my doctor signed me off. When I returned to work, two weeks later, my job had been split between two hospitals three miles apart, which was unnecessary and unacceptable. Eventually I refused to work for her any more and was transferred.

'Although I did stand up for myself, I'm still angry. She's robbed me of many more happy years working in a job I enjoyed with people I liked.'

Laura's story

After starting a new job in the public relations department of an IT company, 36-year-old Laura* ended up in hospital suffering from serious stress disorder. 'I was under so much pressure that within months I was having migraines – something I'd never suffered from before. It wasn't so much that my boss constantly nit-picked, but the fact she wouldn't let me do my job properly. She'd deliberately withhold information so I didn't have time to complete a task, then say it wasn't good enough. Instead of giving up, I tried to beat her, working extra-long hours and reading to improve my technical knowledge, but she continued to criticise me until I felt totally demoralised.

'I was desperately tired. The headaches got worse and I was depressed, covered in eczema and ill with worry, but I didn't dare take time off because I thought it would give her more ammunition. Then, 18 months after I started work, I woke up and my joints had swollen so much I couldn't walk. I was rushed to hospital where I was diagnosed with a stress-related condition and put on steroids. I was off work for six months, during which time my boss went on maternity leave. I tried to go back but I was in tears after only a few hours, so I left for good.

'As a result of the bullying, my self-esteem hit rock bottom, but I've had counselling and now feel I'm getting my life together. It's been a long slog but I wasn't going to let her ruin my life. I've got more confidence now than I've had in ages, plus renewed faith in my ability to do my job. I'm also engaged and back working in PR, but on a freelance basis – I could never be an employee again.'

comes close to reflecting the damage caused to you – is an out-of-court settlement, where the employer wants to minimise publicity.

But there is a glimmer of hope. The MSF's Dignity at Work bill, supported by the TUC, states that an employer is committing a breach of the employee's right to dignity at work if the employee is subject to bullying. The bill covers everything from persistent offensive and intimidating behaviour to unjustified criticism and unreasonable changes to an employee's duties or responsibilities. Although the bill ran out of time in the last parliamentary session, there are plans to reintroduce it in the near future.

In the meantime, one way forward is to fight your own corner. And that's exactly what Rebecca*, who works for a publishing house in the City of London, decided to do when a male colleague, who was one rung higher on the company ladder, started bullying her.

Rebecca confided in another co-worker, who'd witnessed the bully's actions and agreed to help her tackle him. 'Together, we told him how unfair we thought his behaviour was,' says Rebecca. 'It was like watching ice cream melt – he looked so embarrassed and apologetic. He never said another derogatory word to me.'

Where to go for help

- Your trade union (your local branch will be listed in the Yellow Pages).
- For an information sheet and newsletter, write to Workplace Bullying, PO Box 67, Didcot, Oxfordshire OX11 9YS, enclosing an A4 sae and two loose second-class stamps.
- The Andrea Adams Trust (01273 704900) offers advice, mediation and training for companies on ways to prevent bullying.

How to fight it

- Check your job description to see if you're being asked to breach it.
- Keep a diary of all bullying incidents, including what was said and how you felt.
- Keep copies of appraisals.
- Try to get witnesses.
- If the bully has made a disparaging claim against you, send a memo refuting it. Any reply will add to your evidence.
- Take your evidence to your union, welfare or personnel officer and keep your complaint as objective as possible.
- Find out if your employer has a policy on dealing with bullying, and follow company grievance procedures with the help of the body you've approached.
- See your doctor – taking sick leave isn't a sign of weakness.
- Try to get professional counselling or contact a support group.
- If you decide to resign, let the company know you've done so because of bullying.
- Join a relaxation class or concentrate on a hobby – anything that makes you feel positive about yourself again.
- Remember it's the bully's fault, not yours.

* Names have been changed

Good Housekeeping, © *National Magazine Co.*, *November, 2000*

Janet's story

Janet Ballantyne, 54, who was once deputy officer-in-charge of a residential care home in Hamilton, Scotland, fought her bullying case and won £66,000 in an out-of-court settlement.

'I really wasn't interested in financial compensation. I just wanted it on record that my life had been made a misery. I was humiliated in front of colleagues and made to look very small, and my confidence was shattered. Thankfully, my husband was supportive throughout.

'The local representative of my union agreed to help, but the case took ages to come to court and in the meantime I became more and more stressed. I suffered panic attacks and felt very depressed. Finally, a few days before the case was due to start, my lawyers called to say the council were offering a £50,000 settlement. I refused. I'd suffered for four years and wanted them to suffer now. The following morning they offered £66,000 and something snapped. I couldn't take any more and I accepted. I didn't feel jubilant, just relieved that it was over. The woman involved has now left, but that doesn't make me happy either. I'm still on Prozac and have panic attacks. I can't work now and the money is a pittance compared to the value of my old life.'

Beating the workplace bullies

Information from the Institute of Management

Despite the playground rhyme 'sticks and stones may break my bones but words can never hurt me', verbal intimidation can be damaging and is recognised as a form of bullying in the workplace. But the good news is you don't have to put up with it.

Victims of workplace bullying now have access to a range of material to help them deal with the problem. In launching a new publication, *Dealing with Bullying at Work in a Week*, the Institute of Management (IM) and Hodder and Stoughton Educational are adding a concise, accessible guide that employees and managers at all levels will find quick and easy to pick up and use.

The seven-day guide provides daily case studies and action checklists, which identify what bullying is, how to respond to bullying, how to provide support for the bullied and the bully and what the role of the organisation is in dealing with bullying.

It highlights the high costs of bullying for both individuals and organisations. Individuals suffer from stress-related illnesses, mental health problems, poor performance, demotivation and breakdowns. The costs to organisations are reduced efficiency and productivity, lowered motivation and morale, high recruitment and retention costs and potential legal costs.

For individuals the book provides different options for dealing with bullying, such as confronting the bully directly or making an informal or official complaint. It gives guidance on sources of advice and support, such as colleagues and the personnel department inside an organisation and, externally, trade unions, professional associations and Citizens' Advice Bureaux.

To beat the workplace bully the book gives advice on how organisations can develop, publish and monitor a bullying policy, put procedures in place to deal with complaints, train managers on the issues involved and set up helplines for those being bullied.

Dealing with Bullying at Work in a Week is part of the *Successful in a Week* series giving handy and accessible advice on all types of management issues. The *In a Week* books are available at airports, railway stations and motorway service stations, as well as in high street book shops, price £6.99.

Step-by-step guide for beating the bullies:

1. Seek proof of the bullying from the moment you identify it.
2. Find out whether your employer has a policy on bullying or harassment.
3. Log every incident, recording times, dates and witnesses present.
4. Explore the possibilities of witness support.
5. Keep all relevant documentation such as memos.
6. Consider secretly recording evidence, but only if you have support from a personnel officer or higher company manager.
7. Consider seeing a solicitor and making a sworn witness statement (affidavit), especially if you are sure that your organisation will not listen to your complaint.

- The Institute of Management represents over 86,000 individual members making it the largest broadly-based management institute in the UK. It also embraces 600 corporate members. The IM exists to promote the art and science of management through research, education and training and objective representation of managers' views and interests. See page 41 for their address details.

ADDITIONAL RESOURCES

You might like to contact the following organisations for further information. Due to the increasing cost of postage, many organisations cannot respond to enquiries unless they receive a stamped, addressed envelope.

ChildLine
2nd Floor Royal Mail Building
50 Studd Street
London, N1 0QW
Tel: 020 7239 1000
Fax: 020 7239 1001
E-mail: reception@childline.org.uk
Web site: www.childline.org.uk
ChildLine is a free, national helpline for children and young people in trouble or danger. Provides confidential phone counselling service for any child with any problem 24 hours a day. Produces publications. Children or young people can phone or write free of charge about problems of any kind to: ChildLine, Freepost 1111, London N1 0BR, Tel: Freephone 0800 1111. Another Freephone number for children living away from home is Freephone 0800 884444 open Mon-Fri 3.30pm-9.30pm and Sat-Sun 2.00 pm-8.00pm.

Graphical, Paper & Media Union (GPMU)
Keys House
63-67 Bromham Road
Bedford, MK40 2AG
Tel: 01234 351521
Fax: 01234 358558
E-mail: general@gpmu.org.uk
Web site: www.gpmu.org.uk
The Graphical, Paper & Media Union is the world's largest media trade union, and has a membership of over 200,000 working in the print, publishing, paper, IT and media industries in both the UK and the Republic of Ireland.

The Institute of Management
3rd Floor, 2 Savoy Court
Strand
London, WC2R 0EZ
Tel: 020 7497 0580
Fax: 020 7497 0463
Web site: www.inst-mgt.org.uk

The Institute of Management (IM) is the UK's leading professional body for managers. It embraces 89,000 individual members and 560 corporate partners, representing approximately three million employees, making it the largest broadly based management institute in the UK.

Kidscape Campaign for Children's Safety
2 Grosvenor Gardens
London, SW1W 9TR
Tel: 020 7730 3300
Fax: 020 7730 7081
E-mail: info@kidscape.org.uk
Web site: www.kidscape.org.uk
Works to prevent the abuse of children through education programmes involving parents and teachers. Produces a wide range of books, videos and leaflets on child-related issues including bullying and child abuse. Ask for their publications list. Excellent parent and student guides for identifying and dealing with bullying on all levels. Bullying helpline available on 020 7730 3300. Bullying counsellor available 10-4pm weekdays, also advice for parents about helping their children.

Royal College of Psychiatrists
17 Belgrave Square
London, SW1X 8PG
Tel: 020 7235 2351
Fax: 020 7235 1935
E-mail: rcpsych@rcpsych.ac.uk
Web site: www.rcpsych.ac.uk
Produces an excellent series of free leaflets on various aspects of mental health. Supplied free of charge but a stamped, addressed envelope is required.

The Scottish Council for Research in Education (SCRE)
15 St John Street
Edinburgh, EH8 8JR
Tel: 0131 557 2944
Fax: 0131 556 9454
E-mail: scre@scre.ac.uk
Web site: www.scre.ac.uk/bully
The Scottish Council for Research in Education (SCRE) is an independent national body. SCRE provides research, evaluation and training services under contract and expert gateways to educational research in Scotland.

The Suzy Lamplugh Trust
14 East Sheen Avenue
London, SW14 8AS
Tel: 020 8392 1839
Fax: 020 8392 1830
E-mail: trust@suzylamplugh.org
Web site: www.suzylamplugh.org
The Suzy Lamplugh Trust is the national charity for personal safety. It aims to create a safer society and enable people to live safer lives, providing practical personal safety advice for everyone, everyday, everywhere. For free information on bullying, send sae to the Trust at the above address.

Trades Union Congress – Equal Rights Department (TUC)
Congress House
23-28 Great Russell Street
London, WC1B 3LS
Tel: 020 7636 4030
Fax: 020 7636 0632
E-mail: info@tuc.org.uk
Web site: www.tuc.org.uk
The TUC has over 75 member trade unions, representing nearly seven million people from all walks of life. They are Britain's largest voluntary organisation. They campaign on concerns in the world of work and build links with all political parties, business and the community.

INDEX

★★★★★

The Internet has been likened to shopping in a supermarket without aisles. The press of a button on a Web browser can bring up thousands of sites but working your way through them to find what you want can involve long and frustrating on-line searches.

And unfortunately many sites contain inaccurate, misleading or heavily biased information. Our researchers have therefore undertaken an extensive analysis to bring you a selection of quality Web site addresses.

ChildLine
www.childline.org.uk
ChildLine is the UK's free national helpline for children and young people in trouble or danger. Click on the Children and Young People button and go to the Factsheets section of their web site for a range of useful factsheets on various aspects of bullying.

NSPCC – National Society for the Prevention of Cruelty to Children
www.nspcc.org.uk
Click on the Homepage button, then the Search button. Enter to word 'bullying' will bring up a range of NSPCC articles on the issue.

Kidscape Campaign for Children's Safety
www.kidscape.org.uk
Click on Help If Your Child Is Being Bullied. A useful article including a list of contact organisations .

Graphical, Paper & Media Union (GPMU)
www.gpmu.org.uk
Enter the word 'bullying' in their Search field for various articles and press releases on bullying in the workplace.

Success Unlimited
www.successunlimited.co.uk
The UK's most comprehensive resource on bullying and related issues. Essential for student research on virtually all aspects of bullying.

Bully B'ware Productions
www.bullybeware.com
A Canadian site but useful as a comparison on bullying issues in other countries.

BBC Broadcasting Corporation (BBC)
www.bbc.co.uk
Entering the word 'bullying' in the Search filed brings up a rang e of informative articles.

pupiline.net
www.pupiline.net
Enter the word 'bullying' for lots of relevant articles.

Bullying OnLine
www.bullying.co.uk
A useful and informative site on a range of bullying-related issues.

ACKNOWLEDGEMENTS

The publisher is grateful for permission to reproduce the following material.

While every care has been taken to trace and acknowledge copyright, the publisher tenders its apology for any accidental infringement or where copyright has proved untraceable. The publisher would be pleased to come to a suitable arrangement in any such case with the rightful owner.

Chapter One: Bullying at School

Bullying, © ChildLine, The emotional cost of bullying, © Royal College of Psychiatrists, Bullying, © Kidscape, School children fear bullying and violence, © Market & Opinion Research International (MORI), Schoolbully.com, © Amy Cox, One-third of children are 'bullying' victims, © The Daily Mail, 2000, Fear of being bullied, © Schools Health Education Unit (SHEU), Blair backs teenager's cyberwar on bullies, © The Daily Mail, 2000, pupiline.net, © pupiline.net, Every week, 2,300 children become classroom victims, © The Independent Newspaper Ltd, 2000, Beating the bully, © Jerome Monahan, Stop bullies or pay price, schools told, © The Daily Mail, 2000, Take action against bullying, © Bully B'ware, Brothers, sisters and friends, © The Scottish Council for Research in Education (SCRE), Standing up to bullies, © Crown copyright is reproduced with the permission of the Controller of Her Majesty's Stationery Office, Preventing racist bullying, © Kidscape, How young people can help schools tackle bullying, © Anti-Bullying Network.

Chapter Two: Bullying in the Workplace

Bullying in the workplace, © The Suzy Lamplugh Trust, Prevalence of workplace bullying, © UMIST, Insecurity 'fuels job bullying epidemic', © Guardian Newspapers Limited, 2000, Witnessing workplace bullying, © Trades Union Congress (TUC), Bullying, © The Industrial Society, Employees bullied in past six months, © UMIST, The low down: workplace bullying, © Guardian Newspapers Limited, 2000, Workplace bullies pile on the agony, © 2000, Grant Thornton, Please sir, you're a bully, © Jim Pollard, How to . . . recognise a bully, © Guardian Newspapers Limited, 2000, Occupational bullying, © Carole Spiers Associates. International Occupational Stress Consultancy, Bullying survey – response, © UMIST, 'Submissive worriers' the likely victims of bullying at work, © Guardian Newspapers Limited, 2000, Most frequent, regular negative acts, © UMIST, Passive bullying, © The Daily Mail, 2000, Spotting the signs, © Graphical Paper Media Union (GPMU), Bullying in workplace is costing UK £2bn per year, © The Independent Newspaper Ltd, 2000, Half the population are bullied, © Tim Field, Getting to grips with bullying, © Graphical Paper Media Union (GPMU), Why bullying at work has to stop, © National Magazine Co., Beating the workplace bullies, © The Institute of Management.

Photographs and illustrations:

Pages 1, 10, 17, 20, 27, 37, 40: Pumpkin House, pages 3, 7, 13, 15, 18, 21, 23, 33, 38: Simon Kneebone.

Craig Donnellan
Cambridge
January, 2001